"In 1734, at the beginning of the Connecticut Valley revival that ushered in the Great Awakening, Jonathan Edwards preached on the controversial doctrine of justification. Critics found 'great fault' with him for 'meddling' with it, and he 'was ridiculed by many elsewhere.' So today, those who engage in discussions about the nature of justification may find themselves the objects of criticism and ridicule, but the subject is a vital one, precisely because it has been and remains divisive. And it is particularly important in understanding Edwards, because his view on justification has been hotly debated. This volume combines informed historical context and contemporary appropriation, with the aim of considering Edwards 'responsibly and correctly.' What emerges is a balanced assessment of Edwards as an orthodox thinker, yet one with 'creativity, spice, and derring-do.'"

Kenneth P. Minkema, Executive Editor and Director, Jonathan Edwards Center at Yale University

"This superb collection of essays provides insight and guidance not only for understanding the thought of Jonathan Edwards in his historical context, but for wrestling with the current debate regarding the doctrine of justification by faith. This volume will prove to be richly rewarding, theologically engaging, and spiritually edifying for students and scholars alike. Josh Moody is to be commended for bringing together this outstanding group of scholars for such a timely and thoughtful exploration of this important subject. I highly recommend this book."

David S. Dockery, President, Union University

"A significant work that advances the growing scholarship on Jonathan Edwards and contributes to the current debates on justification. These lucid essays demonstrate that the great biblical and Reformation teaching on justification is not a stale, dusty doctrine, but has ramifications for the vitality of the church and the reform of society."

Dennis P. Hollinger, President and Colman M. Mockler Distinguished Professor of Christian Ethics, Gordon-Conwell Theological Seminary

Jonathan Edwards *and* Justification

Jonathan Edwards *and* Justification

Edited by Josh Moody

WHEATON, ILLINOIS

Jonathan Edwards and Justification

Copyright © 2012 by Josh Moody

Published by Crossway
   1300 Crescent Street
   Wheaton, Illinois 60187

Cover design: Dual Identity inc.

First printing 2012

Printed in the United States of America

Trade paperback ISBN: 978-1-4335-3293-1
PDF ISBN: 978-1-4335-3294-8
Mobipocket ISBN: 978-1-4335-3295-5
ePub ISBN: 978-1-4335-3296-2

Library of Congress Cataloging-in-Publication Data

 Jonathan Edwards and justification / edited by Josh Moody.
  p. cm.
 Includes bibliographical references and index.
 ISBN 978-1-4335-3293-1 (tp)
 1. Edwards, Jonathan, 1703–1758. 2. Justification (Christian theology). I. Moody, Josh.
BX7260.E3J64   2012
234'.7—dc23   2012001373

Crossway is a publishing ministry of Good News Publishers.

VP		21	20	19	18	17	16	15	14	13	12
15	14	13	12	11	10	9	8	7	6	5	4	3	2	1

Contents

Editor's Preface

Writing a book with collaboration adds its share of joys, and potential stresses, but I can say clearly that writing with these colleagues has been entirely joyful and not stressful in the least. I am glad to have been able to work together on this project and to be able to see the fruit of so much expertise brought forward for this common cause of examining Edwards's view of justification.

As always when I write on Edwards I am personally conscious of several particular debts of gratitude. I remember with ongoing fondness and appreciation the support, friendship, and collegial counsel of one of the maestros of contemporary Edwards scholars, Kenneth Minkema. His work at Yale University over the years has gone a long way to reviving our interest in Edwards as well as providing the forum for exploring that interest through the expert publication of the Yale volumes on Edwards. I am grateful for his suggestions regarding this volume and his support of it as we got nearer to completion. There are also several friends who many years ago encouraged me to consider Edwards as a serious intellectual sparring partner, and I want to mention, if not all by name at least by group, this relatively large collection of friends and contemporaneous scholars who encouraged me to delve into technical Edwards scholarship. The Whitefield Institute, as it then was, provided much of the "showing the ropes" expertise for my initial forays into this world. And my supervisor at Cambridge, Dr. Thompson, mentored me in the world of accurate, deliberate, and first-rate theological history.

Specifically for this book I wish to thank Lane Dennis at Crossway for his support of this volume's publication. It is a treasure to have such a strong theological vision behind Crossway, and I rejoice with his ministry. Thank you, too, to Tara Davis for her hard work in copyediting the manuscript for Crossway. I also wish to thank Pauline Epps. As I am writing, Pauline is just a few days away from retiring. She has served as executive assistant for my predecessor at College Church, Kent Hughes, and before him Erwin Lutzer at Moody Church. Pauline has provided support for many years for preaching and writing ministries of many in fairly prominent roles of public ministry, and I know that I speak for all who have benefited from her service to the Lord when I say that her work has been appreciated immensely, and has borne much fruit. Thank you, Pauline, and thank you to her husband Dick whose ministry at Moody Bible Institute was massively influential, too. I also wish to thank Carolyn Litfin, my executive assistant, who is such an example of ministry excellence, and whose assistance on this book was invaluable.

No preface would be complete without the traditional mention of the author's (or in this case the editor's) family. Rochelle is a gift beyond compare in this world, and we rejoice together with ministries such as this book and other opportunities to serve Jesus. I want specifically to dedicate this book to one of my children: Sophia. I will dedicate the next book to one of our other children, and somehow manage to keep the whole thing in strict rotation!

On behalf of all those who have contributed to this book, I wish to say simply may we receive the commendation of Jesus: "well done, good and faithful servant(s)." It has been a great joy working together with you.

Before you now you have quite a treat. We have put together a small team of internationally reputed Edwards scholars simply to ask and answer the question, what is Edwards's doctrine of justification? Getting justification right has proven to be difficult, for some more than others, over the last decade or so, and what Edwards thinks, or would have thought about, is not a matter with small significance for the preaching of the gospel or the health of the church. So prepare to look at justification through the eyes of America's greatest theologian, and by that means reengage with the biblical story about how we are made right with God.

JM

Introduction

Josh Moody

You will find much of what I want to say specifically about justification, and Edwards's view of it, in chapter 1, "Edwards and Justification Today." The purpose then of this introductory chapter is twofold. First, I introduce you to the contributors in this volume, if they are not already familiar to you, and prepare the way for their chapters to shine on their own merits. Second, I wish to make it clear in the most general terms why Edwards must still be considered today by all who take the life of the contemporary church seriously, and why in particular we must grasp his view on justification as we preach the gospel, study it, and seek to live by it.

So because I aim to be a thorough nontraditionalist in this book, let me begin in reverse order and start by explaining why Edwards must still be studied today and why in particular his relation to justification is important.

There has been a fair glut of Edwards work recently, it must be acknowledged. In fact, not all works on Edwards are so recent, but because of the prominent ministries of well-known American Christian leaders who look to Edwards for inspiration, the exposure to Edwards at a popular level is more obvious recently. If you examine bibliographies of Edwards scholarship, you will see that ever since Perry Miller's landmark biography at the middle of the last century there has been an upswing of interest in Edwards, as Miller rescued him from the caricature of the backwards bigot (though in so doing he also painted a picture of Edwards that may not have been entirely fair to his unashamed Puritan convictions). But while this Edwards resurgence has been going on at a scholarly level for some time, at a popular level it hit the headlines in 2006 with *Christianity Today's* article "Young, Restless, Reformed" by Collin Hansen and the 2008 publication of Hansen's book, *Young, Restless, Reformed* (with the accompanying image of a "Jonathan Edwards Is My Homeboy" T-shirt), and the ongoing young, restless, and reformed movement that is in play in various other avenues of ministry.

So the question must be asked, and answered in a way that does not feel like special pleading from someone who has a stake in a publication of a book on Edwards, do we really need another book on Edwards?

I think the answer is yes, and defensibly yes on almost any subject that Edwards addresses, because (1) it is always good to read great Christian forebears, such as Augustine or Edwards, and (2) because Edwards was writing in response to the secular Enlightenment, and the greatest need of the contemporary church today is to formulate a theological vision that effectively (also affectively, but that's another story) answers the charge that Christianity is about as up-to-date as the bubonic plague. If we are to find the answer to that challenge, we will find it in Holy Scripture, not in Edwards, or at least that is my conviction as an unembarrassed holder to the doctrine espoused in 2 Timothy 3:16. But while we will find it in Scripture, we may also find that useful conversation partners, such as Edwards, will point us to parts of the Bible that we may have otherwise ignored. Edwards will no doubt be particularly good at this for he was dealing with the source of the Nile of secularization, and we are some way further down trying to work out what to do with it all.

Now to the specific matter of justification. While I think it is defensible that any amount of Edwards studies is a good thing, partly because he was a theological genius, partly because he was dealing with matters that are particularly pertinent today, I believe that we are especially rewarded by paying attention to what Edwards thought about justification.

If you are a theologian, scholar, pastor, preacher, or thinking and reading Christian, you would have had to be living under a rock somewhere, or in some blissful haven on a Pacific Island, not to be aware that there has been a bit of a controversy over justification in recent years. Edwards has been marshaled from time to time as someone who might give support to one idea or another along that controversy. Because of Edwards's authority as a theologian, it is, of course, important that we understand carefully what he thinks about justification.

What the essays before us show is that Edwards's view on justification was as thoroughly orthodox (or not, depending on your point of view) as Calvin's or Luther's. Yet, as ever, Edwards with his orthodoxy has more than a little dash of creativity, spice, and derring-do. That creativity can set you off in the wrong direction unless you consider carefully Edwards's overall work and writing, and put him faithfully and properly into historical context. So it is important not only to consider Edwards, not only to think about what he said regarding justification, but also to do so responsibly and correctly, such as this book tries to achieve.

In addition, as the contributors to this volume make clear, it is important not to do away with Edwards's creativity as a barnacle on an otherwise exemplary individual, as if we were saying, "Thanks Edwards for being orthodox; no thanks for being interesting." Instead, we must not only take heart that creativity is not the foe of orthodoxy; we also need to look at some of the areas of exploration to which he points as models for us to develop a better view of justification, one that can stand the test of time and provide answers to some of the questions that have been raised contemporaneously.

In particular, Edwards's view on justification explores the importance of what is normally called our "position" in Christ. That we are "in" him is surely the crucial area that has to be considered, the area that Paul clearly says was at stake when he wrote to the Galatians: "For through the law I died to the law, so that I might live to God. I have been crucified with Christ. It is no longer I who live, but Christ who lives in me. And the life I now live in the flesh I live by faith in the Son of God, who loved me and gave himself for me. I do not nullify the grace of God, for if righteousness were through the law, then Christ died for no purpose" (Gal. 2:19–21).

Unpacking that paragraph requires studying the rest of Galatians, or at the very least accepting the notion that by putting my faith in Christ I not only receive as something external the righteousness of God, but *in doing that* I become in him, and he in me, "Christ who lives in me." This idea is very different from the traditional Roman Catholic idea that justification is gradually achieved, but it is also rather different from (probably the caricature of) the view that righteousness moves across to us like a gas moves across the room. Instead, righteousness, alien righteousness to use the technical term, is ours purely by faith, and with that, we are in Christ!

Now, I will give the game away if I explore too much more of what that means for Edwards, as the rest of the chapters in this book do that. But it is worth pausing and realizing that when Edwards talks about infusion and the like, what he is referring to is not the infusion of righteousness that the Westminster divines spoke against, but rather the experience of the new creation, the experience of having Christ in us, and us being in him. This supernatural event takes place when someone becomes a Christian—that is what Edwards is describing—and it is what rescues justification from the dusty tomes of the law court exegesis to the living entity that is in biblical thought, and in the experience of millions.

If I stay on this topic much longer, I will begin to turn this academic-level consideration into an altar call, because, of course, as we consider these things with our minds, it is impossible to not at the same time realize their considerable importance for every aspect of our being. In a book on Edwards I dare not use the jaded language of "head" and "heart," for Edwards rightly assures us through his writings consistently that biblical epistemology is not so bifurcated. That is a theme for another book, and I have touched on it in a couple of my previous ones from time to time, but it is enough to say here that when I say that through faith in Christ I experience his righteousness, and this means that I am in him—well, the bells of the church should ring, the hair on the back of your neck stand on end, a shock of thrill run down your spine. There is simply no other subject that is more important for the winning of heaven and the avoiding of hell, and if you get no further in this book than this paragraph, and you take this paragraph to heart (*pace* Edwards), then you have more glory than, I am afraid, countless others who stand on their own religious merits and not on the merit of Christ and his death on the cross.

I want then to whet your appetite for what is to follow. First, my chapter explores the theme of how Edwards's view of justification intersects with some contemporary debates. In doing so it overviews Edwards's view on justification, corrects some common misapprehensions about that view erroneously drawn from his "Miscellanies," and analyzes his better-known writings on the topic, before relating all this in some brevity, but hopefully fecundity, to various well-known more recent conundrums on the topic.

Then comes Kyle Strobel's chapter on participation in justification. In some ways this is the heart of the matter on the technical side of understanding Edwards's view on justification, and Strobel expertly guides us through the relevant material with a deft hand and a sure touch. Rhys Bezzant then broadens the debate to consider the implications of Edwards's doctrine of justification for a social vision. An extraordinarily creative thinker himself, Bezzant connects Edwards's work on justification with his other themes regarding his social vision in ways that portray avenues of great beneficent rewards. Samuel T. Logan Jr. does his excellent work on Edwards's definition of being a Christian in relation to his topic of justification, and with a winsome touch and insightful scholarship shows us how important it is that we connect these two and get them right in Edwards's thinking. Finally, Douglas A. Sweeney asks the question about Edwards's doctrine of justification and presents to us a remarkably vibrant and fulsome depiction of Edwards's doctrine of justification, drawing on areas of Edwards's writing that have not been properly considered previously.

I thank all the contributors for producing such a feast of intellectual consideration and clear exposition of Edwards's world and writing. Read on.

CHAPTER ONE

Edwards and Justification Today

Josh Moody

There has been considerable discussion about Edwards's view of justification in recent years. There has also been a feisty series of interactions about the doctrine of justification itself in contemporary theology. The interplay of the two is not by happenstance, of course, as Edwards (often claimed to be the greatest American theologian) is a bit like Michael Jordan: if you can get him on your side, you have a better chance of winning, or at least of slam dunking on your theological opponent.

The reason why justification is a hot-button issue is essentially straightforward. Justification has been the defining doctrine of Protestantism ever since the Reformation of the sixteenth century, so anyone who wants to redefine Protestantism or the Reformation must tackle this particular doctrine. But the reason why justification has *today* become a matter of debate is a little more complex. For some, apparently, it needs to be discussed in order to make significant progress in Protestant/Roman Catholic ecumenical dialogue (and if progress in such dialogue is not what you want, then the doctrine needs to be underlined and kept entrenched). For others the notion of "justification by faith alone," as traditionally formulated, has become unwarranted due to some technical work on the background of the New Testament, especially by E. P. Sanders. Then into the fray comes the general feeling that much of at least Western Protestantism has become a little superficial, and there seems an implicit agenda in some of the discussion to find room for "works" within Protestant thinking and thereby into Protestant living.

And no doubt there are other rationales, streams of discussion, and various forms of argumentation. The doctrine of justification more generally is discussed today in the works of James Dunn and N. T. Wright, among others. Those who are counterarguing for a more traditional position are rarely found in exalted academic ivory towers, except for Simon Gathercole of Cambridge University. Specifically within Edwards studies, the discussions are found in Thomas A. Schafer's article in *Church History*, Anri Morimoto's book, George Hunsinger's writings, some parts of McDermott's monograph, and, arguing the more conservative position, Samuel T. Logan Jr.'s article.[1] If academic debates were won by sheer weight of numbers, then those who argue that Edwards basically takes a traditional view of justification would be in trouble.

Edwards's doctrine of justification is articulated in three areas of his work: his *quaestio* MA thesis essay, his *Justification by Faith Alone* lectures of 1735, and various entries in his "Miscellanies" unpublished writings. This book will examine each of these areas and determine what exactly was Edwards's doctrine of justification, to what extent was it traditional Reformation thought, and whether the form of the doctrine that Edwards expressed has any relevance to contemporary discussions about justification. This chapter will give an overview of Edwards and justification today. Each of the succeeding chapters will analyze in detail the different areas where Edwards articulates his understanding of justification, taking the form of text and commentary upon the text.

I argue that Edwards's view of justification is relevant today because it articulates the Protestant Reformation view of justification in a way that addresses some of the contemporary questions that are posed to that view. I will first look at Edwards's view of

---

[1] Thomas A. Schafer, "Jonathan Edwards and Justification by Faith," *Church History* 20 (Dec. 1951); Anri Morimoto, *Jonathan Edwards and the Catholic Vision of Salvation* (University Park, PA: Pennsylvania State University Press, 1995); George Hunsinger, "Dispositional Soteriology: Jonathan Edwards on Justification by Faith Alone," *Westminster Theological Journal* 66 (2004): 107–20; Gerald R. McDermott, *Jonathan Edwards Confronts the Gods: Christian Theology, Enlightenment Religion, and Non-Christian Faith* (New York: Oxford University Press, 2000); Samuel T. Logan Jr., "The Doctrine of Justification in the Theology of Jonathan Edwards," *Westminster Theological Journal* 46 (1984): 26–52.

justification, then more briefly at the Reformation Protestant view of justification, and finally at how Edwards's view of justification addresses some of the contemporary questions about justification.

Edwards's View of Justification

Jonathan Edwards has long been recognized as a creative mind, and his formulation of the doctrine of justification is no exception. The crucial issue, however, is whether Edwards's view of justification is creative in form but essentially traditional in content, or whether Edwards's view of justification is creative at both levels. Is Edwards saying something novel (that is "new"), or is he saying something in a novel way? There is a world of difference between the two possibilities, and no reason logically to assume that just because Edwards is *at least* saying something in a new way, he must therefore be saying something new. There is a kind of specious, uneducated cant that is suspicious of anything novel, lest it not be "what was always said." I trust we can all avoid that sort of ancestor worship. And there is a kind of immaturity that looks for the letter not the spirit of an idea, and that once it finds a slightly different formulation believes that the essence has changed. Ironically, of course, the reverse can be true. One can find someone who has a "justification by faith alone" bumper sticker, and talks of imputation of righteousness, propitiation, and all the rest, but actually behind the apparently old-fashioned formulations holds to a completely new set of ideas. What we are looking for here is the spirit of what Edwards is saying, not the letter. We will certainly look at the "letter," the details, but what we need to understand is the message that is being communicated, or to use Edwardsian terminology, we are looking for the idea.

A word about bias: personally, I hold to a rather traditional view of justification by faith alone, though I hope I am able to express it in some interesting, perhaps even at times novel, ways. But I am not committed to finding that Edwards agrees with me. I do not agree with Edwards about everything, perhaps particularly his fascinating eschatology, or his rather invigorating semi-idealist metaphysics. I come to my own views for my own

reasons, and without doubt have long found Edwards a helpful sparring partner in the matter of working out the meaning
of life, the universe, and everything. But he is not my master,
and my world will not be shaken if I find that Edwards really
was a crypto–Roman Catholic. I will say this though: those who
argue that Edwards's view of justification inches him toward a
Catholic view of justification are the ones who have to do all
the legwork. After all at a basic commonsense level it is intrinsi-
cally *unlikely* that Edwards was a pseudo-Roman Catholic. He was,
let's remember, an eighteenth-century Puritan in New England
who, perhaps more than anyone in world history, did not usually
have to defend himself against charges of "going over to Rome."
Still, you never know. And I've come to this discussion with an
open mind.

Discussions about Edwards's teaching on justification focus
primarily on three areas, namely his use of the word "infusion,"
his understanding of the order of salvation, and his discussion
about faith and love.[2] We'll consider each of these in turn.

Edwards's Use of the Word "Infusion"

The word "infusion" stands out because it is used in Roman
Catholic theology to explain a theory of how grace works that
is different from the Protestant theory of how grace works. But
does Edwards use the word in a Roman Catholic (or semi–Roman
Catholic) way, or does he invest in it some meaning of his own?
A third alternative is that he uses it in a non–Roman Catholic
way but a thoroughly traditional Protestant way. Oh the vagaries
of theological lexicography! If I wanted to be really devilish, I
might suggest that he could also have been using a knowingly
Roman Catholic word without intending to import into it our
particular ecumenical sensitivities. Protestants do use Roman
Catholic words frequently ("Trinity," "salvation," etc.) without
necessarily meaning them in Roman Catholic ways, or use them
in Roman Catholic ways, but only when they overlap happily

---

[2] This is the framework that Morimoto adopts in *Jonathan Edwards and the Catholic Vision of Salvation*, 105–30.

with Protestant meaning (such as the word "Trinity"). If the word "infused" *always* meant something irreducibly Roman Catholic, then spotting it in Edwards's writings would certainly set the Protestant scholastics' nerves tingling. But I don't see any reason why it should, and in fact, on closer observation, it does not. This is not like finding Edwards talking approvingly about purgatory, for instance.

Actually, when Edwards uses "infusion," he is talking about regeneration (to use another theological term). He sometimes uses the language of "infusion" in his "Miscellanies"—his unpublished notebooks—when he is discussing how ridiculous he thinks it is to deny that the Holy Spirit can actually come in and change someone's life. Edwards is not attempting an ecumenical dialogue on the topic of justification in any of these "Miscellanies" that I can see (unsurprisingly for someone writing before Vatican II and certainly before Evangelicals and Catholics Together). He is trying intellectually to browbeat the deists of the eighteenth century who wanted their cake and to be able to eat it too; they wanted to have God and rationalism, no miracles, nothing so "weird" as being born again, or grace coming into your life. Edwards talks in fairly repetitive terms throughout his "Miscellanies" about how absurd it is to say that God can do something in your life but that the Holy Spirit cannot be "infused" (or cause regeneration). A few examples should make this obvious:

> Those that deny infusion by the Holy Spirit, must of necessity deny the Spirit to do anything at all. "By the Spirit's infusing" is an unintelligible expression; but however, let be meant what will, those that say there is no infusion contradict themselves. For they say the Spirit doth something in the soul; that is, he causeth some motion, or affection, or apprehension to be in the soul, that at the same time would not be there without him. Now I hope, that God's Spirit doth he doth; he doth so much as he doth, or he causeth in the soul so much as he causeth, let that be how little soever. So much as is purely the effect of his immediate motion, that is the effect of his immediate motion, let that be

what it will; and so much is infused, how little soever that be. This is self-evident.[3]

Edwards is arguing against "those." Who are these people? We, of course, do not know for sure, but almost certainly they are some mixture of those eighteenth-century New England bug-bears, Arminians and/or deists. Surely they are not Reformation Protestants who deny "infusion" *in the sense that* justification is a declaration of righteousness, not an infusion of righteousness. Note that Edwards nowhere here mentions justification.

> To say that a man who has no true virtue and no true grace can acquire it by frequent exercises of [it], is as much a contradiction as to say a man acts grace when he has no grace, or that he has it [when] he has it not. For tell me [how] a man that has no true grace within him shall begin to exercise it: before he begins to exercise it, he must have some of it. How shall [he] act virtuously the first time? How came he by that virtue which he then acted? Certainly not [by] exercise of virtue, for it supposes that he never acted virtuously before, and therefore could not get it by acting of it before.[4]

This is a similar point. Edwards is saying that morality or virtue cannot take place simply by trying hard or developing habits. For there to be an exercise of grace there needs to be grace. Again, no discussion of justification (incidentally, it is common to use "grace" in Puritan and Reformation writings in a wider sense than solely justification).

And in case any wonder whether I am making up the idea that Edwards's use of "infusion" equates to what we more normally discuss under the heading of "regeneration," or that I'm just substituting a term used by Edwards for a term that I might feel more comfortable with, consider two "Miscellanies" on the subject of infusion. First,

---

[3] Jonathan Edwards, "The 'Miscellanies,' no. p," in *The Works of Jonathan Edwards Online* (hereafter *WJE Online*), vol. 13, *The "Miscellanies," a–z, aa–zz, 1–500*, ed. Thomas A. Schafer (Jonathan Edwards Center, Yale University, 2008), 171. On infused grace (early in Edwards's series of "Miscellanies").

[4] "Miscellanies," no. 73, *WJE Online*, 13:242 (on habits).

And seeing it is thus, how analogous hereto is it to suppose that however God has left meaner gifts, qualifications and attainments in some measure in the hands of second causes, that yet true virtue and holiness, which is the highest and most noble of all the qualifications gifts and attainments of the reasonable creature, and is the crown and glory of the human, and that by which he is nearest to God and does partake of his image and nature, and is the highest beauty and glory of the whole creation, and is as it were the life and soul of the soul, *that is given in the new creation or new birth*, should be what God don't leave to the power of second causes, or honor any arm of flesh or created power or faculty to be the proper instrument of, but that he should reserve it in his own hands to be imparted more immediately by himself, in the efficacious operation of his own Spirit.[5]

By "infused grace" Edwards means, he says, what "is given in the new creation or new birth." I am not sure it could be much clearer than that.

Second, in "Miscellanies" 1028 on the same topic, where as typical for his later "Miscellanies" he quotes from various authors and there is less of Edwards's own thoughts on the matter, the author he is reading about "infused grace" is, *"These things above are taken from Dr. Doddridge, On Regeneration, Sermon 7."*[6]

I am tempted to say QED in terms of infusion. But one last point may help: in none of the "Miscellanies" on infusion is justification mentioned. And, out of 1,359 notes or "Miscellanies" on various topics, plus two scales of "Miscellanies" from A–Z (the second time with the notation of "aa," etc.), Edwards wrote eight "Miscellanies" on the subject of infusion. I find this hard to square with Thomas Schafer's confident comment with relation to the "Miscellanies" that, "The conception of regenerating and sanctifying grace as an infusion of new habits and principles is *prominent* in Edwards's writings on the subject."[7] It is a rate of 0.5 percent

---

[5] Jonathan Edwards, "The 'Miscellanies,' no. 1003," in *WJE Online*, vol. 20, The "Miscellanies," 833–1152, ed. Amy Plantinga Pauw (Jonathan Edwards Center, Yale University, 2008), 328. On infused grace; emphasis added.
[6] "Miscellanies," no. 1028, *WJE Online*, 20:366.
[7] Schafer, "Jonathan Edwards and Justification by Faith," n72.

on infusion in the "Miscellanies," which is not what I would call prominent.

Edwards does have some interesting things to say under the topic of justification itself about obedience, but we will turn to that when we consider the general matter of what Edwards called "evangelical obedience."

For now, let us turn to another common discussion concerning Edwards's view of justification: his understanding of the order of salvation.

Edwards's Understanding of the Order of Salvation

If you were to write an *Idiot's Guide* on the distinction between Roman Catholic theology and Protestant theology regarding the matter of the order of salvation, and you were a Protestant, you would simply say that Protestants believe that justification precedes sanctification while Roman Catholics have it the other way around. There's a lot of truth in that statement, even if it would be a summary worthy of the popular "*Idiot's Guide*" series. Given that common distinction, then, when people read various statements in Edwards that indicate he believes that God is at work in a sinner's life before he savingly believes and is justified, some understandably leap to the conclusion that Edwards thereby is overturning this common distinction in terms of the order of salvation.

For instance, Perry Miller, in his seminal biography of Edwards that kick-started much of the modern fascination with Edwards as a towering intellectual giant, noticed this since-frequently-commented-upon phrase in Edwards's *Justification by Faith Alone* lectures: "What is real in the union between Christ and his people, is the foundation of what is legal."[8]

What does Edwards mean by this phrase? Various possibilities present themselves. Edwards *could* mean that he thinks that sanctification precedes justification. From the wording of that phrase

---

[8] Perry Miller, *Jonathan Edwards* (New York: W. Sloane Associates, 1949). Quote can be found in *WJE Online*, vol. 19, *Sermons and Discourses, 1734–1738*, ed. M. X. Lesser (Jonathan Edwards Center, Yale University, 2008).

alone, without paying any attention to the context, both historical and in the actual argument of the lectures themselves, that is a possible interpretation of the phrase. But is it likely? For various reasons we have already suggested—that Edwards was famed as a defender of Reformed orthodoxy, arguing against Arminians, and that there wasn't a Roman Catholic in sight in the heart of Puritan New England as a viable theological opponent—it seems superficially unlikely. But it is possible if we simply take the words themselves without considering their context.

However, if we consider Edwards's words in context, then that interpretation is impossible. The following is a long quotation, but if we want to understand Edwards's view of the "order of salvation," we need to read the context of the phrase that Miller highlighted:

> God don't give those that believe, an union with, or an interest in the Savior, in reward for faith, but only because faith is the soul's active uniting with Christ, or is itself the very act of unition, on their part. God sees it fit, that in order to an union's being established between two intelligent active beings or persons, so as that they should be looked upon as one, there should be the mutual act of both, that each should receive the other, as actively joining themselves one to another. God in requiring this in order to an union with Christ as one of his people, treats men as reasonable creatures, capable of act, and choice; and hence sees it fit that they only, that are one with Christ by their own act, should be looked upon as one in law: what is real in the union between Christ and his people, is the foundation of what is legal; that is, it is something really in them, and between them, uniting them, that is the ground of the suitableness of their being accounted as one by the Judge: and if there is any act, or qualification in believers, that is of that uniting nature, that it is meet on that account that the Judge should look upon 'em, and accept 'em as one, no wonder that upon the account of the same act or qualification, he should accept the satisfaction and merits of the one, for the other, as if it were their satisfaction and merits: it necessarily follows, or rather is implied.
>
> And thus it is that faith justifies, or gives an interest in Christ's satisfaction and merits, and a right to the benefits procured thereby, viz. as it thus makes Christ and the believer one

in the acceptance of the Supreme Judge. 'Tis by faith that we have a title to eternal life, because 'tis by faith that we have the Son of God, by whom life is. The apostle John in those words, 1 John 5:12, "He that hath the Son hath life," seems evidently to have respect to those words of Christ that he gives an account in his gospel. John 3:36, "He that believeth on the Son hath everlasting life, and he that believeth not the Son shall not see life." And in the same places that the Scripture speaks of faith as the soul's "receiving," or "coming to Christ," it also speaks of this receiving, or coming to, or joining with Christ, as the ground of an interest in his benefits: "To as many as received him, to them gave the power to become the sons of God"; "Ye will not come unto me that ye might have life." And there is a wide difference between its being looked on suitable that Christ's satisfaction and merits should be theirs that believe, because an interest in that satisfaction and merit is but a fit reward of faith, or a suitable testimony of God's respect to the amiableness and excellency of that grace, and its only being looked on suitable that Christ's satisfaction and merits should be theirs, because Christ and they are so united, that in the eyes of the Judge they may be looked upon, and taken, as one.[9]

What is Edwards saying? He is saying that the reason God accepts people who believe is because they are united with Christ. This is not merely "legal" but "real," for the basis of their acceptance (or the foundation) is Christ. "Faith justifies . . . as it thus makes Christ and the believer one in the acceptance of the Supreme Judge." Or, by faith, "Christ and they are so united, that in the eyes of the Judge they make be looked upon, and taken, as one."

No doubt if you read various Reformed theologians down through the years you will find some variety on the matter of the "union with Christ," but all we need to notice here is that Edwards is *not* arguing that what is "real" in the believer is their personal sanctification, either in a works righteous semi-Pelagian way or in a Roman Catholic sense (which, for many Reformed theologians, would be similar). Instead he is arguing that what is

---

[9] Ibid., 158–59, http://edwards.yale.edu/archive?path=aHR0cDovL2Vkd2FyZHMueWFsZS5lZHU vY2dpLWJpbi9uZXdwaGlsby9nZXRvmplY3QucGw/Yy4xODo5OjEud2plbw==.

"real" in the believer is the real person of Jesus Christ himself. It is his merits, his righteousness, Christ himself that is "real" and the "foundation of what is legal."

My sense is that the same distinction pertains across Edwards's writings on this matter, both published and unpublished. Another example is from "Miscellanies," no. 77. He is talking about conversion when he says (this is the excerpt that Schafer refers to):

> There must be the principle before there can be the action, in all cases; there must be an alteration made in the heart of the sinner before there can be action consequent upon this alteration; yea, there must be a principle of holiness before holiness is in exercise.[10]

A principle of holiness before holiness is in exercise! Surely this is a tilt toward a more Roman Catholic understanding of the order of salvation? Again, let us read the miscellany in question in context:

> What is held by some, that none can be in a state of salvation before they have particularly acted a reception of the Lord Jesus Christ for a Savior, and that there cannot be sanctification one moment before the exercise of faith, as they have described it, cannot be true, as they explain this reception of Christ. There must be the principle before there can be the action, in all cases; there must be an alteration made in the heart of the sinner before there can be action consequent upon this alteration; yea, there must be a principle of holiness before holiness is in exercise. Yea, this alteration must not only be before this act of faith in nature (as the cause before the effect) but also in time, if this embracing of Christ as a Savior be a successive action, that is, an action where one thought and act of the mind in any wise follows another, as it certainly is.
>
> For first, there must be an idea of Jesus Christ in the mind, that is an agreeable and truly lovely idea to him; but this cannot be before the soul is sanctified. There must also be the acts of true belief, of his willingness to receive, etc.; neither can this be before sanctification. There must also be a hatred of sin before Christ can be received as a Savior from sin; neither can this be

---

[10] *WJE Online*, vol. 13, *The "Miscellanies," Entry Nos. a–z, aa–zz, 1–500*, ed. Thomas A. Schafer (Jonathan Edwards Center, Yale University, 2008), 245.

without sanctification. And after this, there must be the act of embracing; neither is there properly an act of faith, as they explain [it], before this is done. Now these thoughts must succeed one another, whether in this order or not, although it be as quick as one thought can follow another; but sanctification must be in the soul before one of them is in the mind.[11]

What is Edwards talking about? He is discussing the idea that "sanctification" can only come after faith. But, Edwards asks, how can you believe in Jesus Christ, turn from your sins, rejoice in Jesus ("repent and believe") unless you first have some "sanctified" view of Jesus? For Edwards you cannot. This certainly makes Edwards a full-on, hard-core Calvinist, but it does not take him any closer to Rome than Calvin. Edwards is arguing against a more Arminian concept of salvation; he is saying that all must be of God, that God must bring life in the soul. I'm not sure Conrad Cherry was right to say that whenever we see "sanctification" in Edwards we should read "regeneration," but that certainly is more what the word means in this context. Perhaps we should say instead that whenever we read a word in Edwards, we should not override it with our theological distinctions. For Edwards "sanctification" is a more broadly defined word meaning "that which is holy," and certainly Christ in the soul (the "union," remember?), the regeneration, is holy in this sense. We need more sophistication in our theological categories beyond an *Idiot's Guide* definition, because while Calvinists typically think that justification precedes sanctification (in the sense we more commonly mean that word today), they also think that justification is not by faith in the sense of faith as my own personal volitional autonomous will but rather, commonly, that regeneration precedes justification. I suppose we could say that Edwards is saying that the order is (in true *Idiot's Guide* form) "regeneration-justification-sanctification." And it makes Edwards no more Roman Catholic on the order of salvation than John Calvin (or John Owen, Richard Sibbes, and B. B. Warfield for that matter).

---

[11] Ibid.

We need to come to the Reformation Protestant view of justification and analyze it in greater sophistication, but before we do that we must examine one more subset of Edwards's own view of justification: his view on "faith and love." We will also discuss his comments about "evangelical obedience" and "disposition" in relation to justification.

Edwards's Understanding of Faith and Love

Here we come to an area in Edwards's view of justification that is not only complex and strange to modern ears, but also favorable to contemporary followers of Edwards generally. In brief, while the more shrill critics of Edwards's Reformational orthodoxy are occasionally misleading, and certainly incorrect to label him as moving closer to Rome in any of these aspects, underlying Edwards's extended discussions in various parts of his oeuvre, both published and unpublished, is a discussion between him and the Puritan notion of "preparationism." I talk about this elsewhere, but basically Edwards does not, in my view, follow William Perkins or other full-blown "preparationists," nor even the concertinaed distinctions of his grandfather Solomon Stoddard, in the way that he insists that any form of prework of God before faith is gracious.[12] What Edwards is doing is reworking what for him was a traditional view of the pattern of conversion, guarding against what he perceived as the threat of Arminianism, bringing it into line with what were then modern views of the soul and psychology (*à la* Locke), and in short being typically "Edwards-like" in his creativity and orthodoxy. The trouble for most modern "Puritans" is that many would agree with Spurgeon's famous dismissal of any form of preparationism as being unkind, and, many might add, questionably biblical, as well as ineffective evangelistically.

I can't review the whole New England apparatus of preparationism here (the scholarly work on it is that by Pettit),[13] but in

---

[12] Josh Moody, *Jonathan Edwards and the Enlightenment: Knowing the Presence of God* (University Park, PA: Pennsylvania State University Press, 2005), 32–33.

[13] See Norman Pettit, *The Heart Prepared: Grace and Conversion in Puritan Spiritual Life* (New Haven, CT and London: Yale University Press, 1966).

brief, within British, European, and then New England Puritanism there was a stream of thinking that emphasized the need for "preparing" the heart for conversion by various external acts, or inward attitudes. There were discussions as to what extent these acts or attitudes were natural or supernatural in origin, and there lies the rub of what Edwards is discussing. He is insisting that any kind of preparation is supernatural or gracious in origin. If you say that there is a human element to "attending regularly on the means of grace" (going to church, listening to preaching, and such) then you end up saying that some people may seek and not find, which seems counter to the clear teaching of Christ. Or you find ways to distinguish what is real seeking and what is not; in short you tie yourself in knots. And it's those knots that Edwards is seeking to untie with his discussions about faith and love, evangelical obedience, and disposition.

Some of this is helpfully reviewed in Anri Morimoto's work, though unfortunately for Morimoto's case that Edwards was veering toward a Catholic (or at least more "ecumenical") view of justification, the most startling quotation is incorrect.[14] Edwards, Morimoto says, "encounters a standard Protestant criticism of the concept of 'faith informed by love', and wonders in an innocent and unsuspecting tone why it is called 'wicked' and 'wretched.'"[15] Actually, the one who wondered "in an innocent and unsuspecting tone" why Thomas Goodwin is correct to criticize a standard Roman Catholic way for formulating things was not Jonathan Edwards but Jonathan Edwards Jr.[16] Jonathan Edwards Jr. may or may not have been thoroughly traditionally Reformed on justification, but that doesn't have much relevance as to whether Edwards Sr. was.

This brings up a more general point about Edwards's many notebooks and "Miscellanies" from which Edwards scholars love

---

[14] Morimoto, *Jonathan Edwards and the Catholic Vision of Salvation*, 122–23.
[15] Ibid., 123.
[16] The introduction to the Yale volume that includes this complex notebook of Edwards makes this point clear. Incidentally, this volume was edited by Sang Lee from Princeton who seems to have inspired Morimoto's dissertation (on which Morimoto's book is based)—a strange coincidence, but I digress.

to quote. They are fascinating, there are many of them, and they are rich with insights into how Edwards's mind worked. But they can also be dangerous. We must never forget that they were not intended to be published. That they have been is a good thing because they give us insight into the working mind of an undisputed theological genius. But they are not necessarily his fully-formed opinions. It's like looking at Van Gogh's oil paint palate and drawing conclusions about what kind of painting style he believed in. It might give us insight into his method, and we might draw some connections between that and what he painted, but it wouldn't tell us finally what he wanted to paint. Only Edwards's published works, by his own intention, during his own lifetime, reveal with certainty what he wanted to say. Perhaps Edwards has hidden opinions in his notebooks not consistent with his preaching and writing, but the majority of Edwards scholarship has long shown that not to be the case. Each time I engage with fellow Edwards scholars on the "Miscellanies," I make a fresh resolution to comb through all my personal extended notes and jottings on theological matters. If I am to be held to the stake for every semiformulated idea I have ever penned in private journals, I had better get rid of some of them before I pass through the veil.

Now, regarding faith and love, Edwards says:

> 'Tis the same agreeing or consenting disposition that according to the divers objects, different state or manner of exerting, is called by different names. When 'tis exerted towards a Savior, [it is called] faith or trust; when towards one that governs us and orders our affairs for us, faith or trust; when towards one that tells and teaches us, faith or belief; when towards a Savior, a governor and instructor (or a king, priest and prophet) in one, by no other name than faith; when towards doctrines, whether of things past, present or to come, faith or belief; when towards unseen good things promised, faith and also hope; when towards a gospel or good news, faith; when towards persons excellent, love; when towards commands, obedience; when towards God with respect to changes, 'tis properly called resignation; when with respect to calamities, submission. Believing must be to the degree of trust before it is saving. Though unregenerate men

may in some measure believe the gospel, yet they don't believe it so that they dare to trust to it; they are not willing to perform its prescriptions, trusting to its offers, which is true believing in Christ. And surely good works are supported by such a faith.[17]

This is certainly interesting. Edwards is saying that faith can be called by different names. Elsewhere (in his notebook concerning faith) he has a great list of biblical references for faith being also called "hope" in various places. Here he is saying that underneath these different names for the same thing is a "consenting disposition." What does he mean by that?

One scholar concludes that "what Edwards finally teaches is justification by disposition alone."[18] That's clever, because Edwards does talk about this foundational disposition in various places, but I am not sure it's quite fair. Nor is it fair to say, as the same scholar goes on (in an attempt to explain the divergence of opinion on Edwards on this matter), that your thoughts on this matter depend on what kind of "focus" you bring to your interpretation of Edwards and justification. If you bring a "soft focus," you see him as Reformed. If you bring a "crisper focus," you get a different picture. No, it is not a matter of wanting to view Edwards through a "soft focus lens," like you might want to view your favorite grandmother through a soft focus lens for a family portrait. Edwards, like Oliver Cromwell, deserves to be painted "warts and all." But we're just getting the wrong wart. He is attempting to wring the best of his heritage of preparationism (making it gracious), *not* pseudo–Roman Catholicism.

You will see something similar when you read Edwards on his subject of "evangelical obedience." Again, those who are looking for some sort of "works-righteousness" or a more Roman Catholic understanding of works in the Christian life latch onto this term and see it as justification (if you will excuse the pun) for making Edwards in that image. In reality, Edwards is saying that just because he believes in justification by faith alone, that does not

---

[17] "Miscellanies," no. 218, *WJE Online*, 13:344–45 (on faith justifying).
[18] Hunsinger, "Dispositional Soteriology," 119.

mean he thinks that those who are so justified need not obey. He calls this—with deliberate care, I think—"*evangelical* obedience," not in the sense of the modern "evangelical" movement, of course, but playing on the heritage of Reformation Protestants who were thought in the German sense to be self-designated as "evangelicals," and (equally of course), playing on his understanding of the gospel, or in Greek the "*evangel*," to say that this gospel of his really does produce good works.

So in his *Justification by Faith Alone* lectures he is concerned to show "how evangelical obedience is concerned in this affair," that is, how obeying God comes out of a doctrine when you are justified by faith alone. This is addressed in section 3 of his "doctrine," and when he comes to section 4 (answering objections), the objections he deals with are mostly about obedience of one kind or another. This does not mean that Edwards needs to defend his "novel" doctrine of justification against slippage toward a more Roman Catholic view of justification. What it means is that every time anyone has ever preached "justification by faith *alone*," the comeback is, "Well, what about all those times in the Bible where it says that works are important?" That's the shape of the argument.

Or, in his *Charity and Its Fruits* series of lectures, he describes how love is the summary of all the virtues. Don't get excited; that doesn't mean that Edwards thinks that "faith works through love" in a Roman Catholic sense. So he says at one point that love "belongs to [faith's] essence."[19] This is different from saying that love is the essence of faith,[20] in the same way that I can belong to the essence of an organization without *being* its essence. Although elsewhere Edwards does say that love is the essence of faith, it seems as if the difference between the two expressions does not loom large in the grander scheme of his thinking on

---

[19] *WJE* Online, vol. 8, *Ethical Writings*, ed. Paul Ramsay (Jonathan Edwards Center, Yale University, 2008), 330.
[20] Which is more how Morimoto seems to interpret it here. See *Jonathan Edwards and the Catholic Vision of Salvation*, 122.

this matter.[21] But part of Edwards's argument most generally that these virtues of the Christian are *concatenated* together: they are a chain, specifically, more than a connection. This is his way of explaining the "greatest of these is love" thesis from the passage upon which he is commenting, 1 Corinthians 13. This concatenation is attractive as an idea, perhaps helpful, or intriguing. It may reformulate the Christian idea of ethics away from a more heavy preparationist way of looking at spirituality; it may defend a justification by faith alone position against its classic critique that it leaves the door open to immorality. These may be its virtues, or its warts, depending on your opinion. But I can't see why, logically, saying that love belongs to or is the essence of faith (surely an emphasis on love few Christians would want to disagree with, given Christ's summary of the greatest commandments), or that love is the summation of all the virtues, makes Edwards any more Roman Catholic than Jesus or Paul—which is perhaps to beg the question at another level, but that's a different matter. The one eye directed toward the criticism of justification, and Edwards's repositioning of preparationism, do make his doctrine feel a little "puritanical" to me (for want of a much better expression). But I think that's about as far as we can go in terms of saying that Edwards moved from a classic Reformation Protestant view.

Having looked then at Edwards's view of justification and found it not to be persuasively inching toward Roman Catholicism, but rather formulated to emphasize the doctrine of justification in a non-Arminian, non-Stoddardean, preparationist, and rather creative way ("concatenation"), we are brought to the next stage in the strange matter of Edwards as the purportedly crypto–Roman Catholic: And that is the rather shocking lack of familiarity that many modern scholars have of Puritan and ecclesiastical history toward the central doctrines that such Puritans and/or Christian

---

[21] "Miscellanies," no. 820: "Love is of the essence of faith, yea, is the very life and soul of it, and the most essential thing in it," *WJE Online*, vol. 18, *"The Miscellanies," Entry Nos. 501–832*, ed. Ava Chamberlain (Jonathan Edwards Center, Yale University, 2008), 531.

leaders at the time held. So let's consider then the Reformation Protestant view of justification.

Reformation Protestant View of Justification

I was again alerted to this quite recently when reading a very good historian of another period of the Reformation and Puritan period, and his fascinating portrayal of the young Queen Elizabeth. At one point in the book, as an arresting but somewhat throwaway comment, this historian claimed that the doctrine of justification by faith alone is something that "the average first year under-graduate would struggle to understand." I suspect he is right. But I think we need to take that insightful comment further and—with all due respect—say that apparently the doctrine of justification by faith alone is something that some otherwise first-rate and reputed scholars struggle to understand. At least, I'm beginning to come to that conclusion the more I read works on justification. I read some literature that apparently brilliantly criticizes the Reformation Protestant view of justification and think, fine, but what does that have to do with the *actual* Reformation Protestant view of justification? Of course, those who are particularly well-schooled in the Reformation Protestant view of justification are often not scholars of historical repute, so we then appear to have a situation where one group is simply talking at cross-purposes with another.

This is all the more remarkable because in Puritan New England times, the doctrine of justification by faith alone was not something deemed to be particularly complex intellectu-ally. It was the kind of idea that your average seven-year-old was expected to grasp fully, having engaged with the classic catechism on the matter from a very young age.

Now put all that together and you have quite an explosive mix of confusion. One group, very sensitive to the vagaries of the discussion about justification, another group viewing it as some diabolically complex intellectual idea, both studying people who assumed that its basic message was simple enough that the seven-year-olds in their congregation did not need to have it explained.

So where do you go for the authority on what is the Reformation Protestant view of justification? That is a little tricky. Some would quote from a creedal statement, like the Westminster Confession of Faith. Others would quote from Calvin or Luther. Part of the problem is that for Reformation Protestants the only authority is Scripture, but—scholars realize—Roman Catholics in particular have a different interpretation of many scriptural texts. Another problem is that some love to use complex sounding phrases, often in Latin (*simul iustus et peccator* is a particular favorite at the moment), to explain the doctrine of justification. This is ironic, given that part of the *raison d'être* (See! French!) of the Reformation movement was to bring religion into the language of the people. (Shall we say lingua franca?) Even the doctrine itself has a lovely Latin term: *sola fide*.

We will use them all: Bible, Luther, Calvin, and the Westminster Confession. We are going to start with the Bible because for all Reformation Protestants, what Luther, Calvin, or any Protestant confession says must submit to the authority of Scripture—*sola Scriptura*. (It just sounds better in Latin.)

The classic biblical texts are the letter to the Galatians and the letter to the Romans. Edwards's *Justification by Faith Alone* lectures are from Romans 4:5. Luther's lectures on Galatians were seminal for the Reformation movement. We will examine a quotation from Galatians then Romans (and remember these texts are *the* authority for all the Reformation Protestants, including Edwards, on the subject of justification, which is why we need to quote them to understand what Reformation Protestants believe).

> I do not frustrate the grace of God: for if righteousness come by the law, then Christ is dead in vain. (Gal. 2:21 KJV)

> But to him that worketh not, but believeth on him that justifieth the ungodly, his faith is counted for righteousness. (Rom. 4:5 KJV)

People have discussed these two texts ad infinitum, but to get a sense of how Protestants classically have understood them, let us hear from Luther and Calvin.

Luther on Galatians 2:21:

[Paul] simply says: "If justification were through the Law, etc."
Therefore human reason with the assistance of laws, even of
divine ones, cannot achieve righteousness but snatches a man
away from righteousness and rejects Christ. But if it could
achieve righteousness, then Christ would have died to no purpose. Therefore you oppose the death of Christ to every single
Law; and, with Paul, you know nothing except Christ and Him
crucified (1 Cor. 2:2), so that nothing except Him may shine. Then
you will be learned, righteous, and holy; and you will receive the
Holy Spirit, who will preserve you in the purity of the Word and
of faith. But once Christ is lost sight of, everything is pointless.[22]

Calvin on Romans 4:5:

Here again God is said to justify us while He freely forgives sinners
and favors with His love those with whom He might justifiably
be angry, i.e. while His mercy abolishes our unrighteousness.[23]

Anyone can interpret Luther and Calvin on these verses as
they will, but it seems clear that their main point is that God
declares righteous those who believe, irrespective of any good
works or moral actions they perform in the widest possible sense.
That last phrase "in the widest possible sense" is crucial for understanding the debate around the interpretation of these passages,
where before (and more recently) many have thought that Paul
was referring solely to the ceremonial law. Much of the discussion
about the Protestant view of justification focuses on criticizing it
and defending it, which, though understandable, can cloud its
basic and fairly simple meaning. Consider what the Westminster
Confession says regarding justification:

Those whom God effectually calls, He also freely justifies; not by
infusing righteousness into them, but by pardoning their sins,

---

[22] Martin Luther, "Lectures on Galatians," in *Luther's Works*, American Edition (55 vols.; ed. Jaro-
slav Pelikan and Helmut T. Lehmann; Philadelphia: Muehlenberg and Fortress, and St. Louis:
Concordia, 1955–1986), 26:184.
[23] John Calvin, *New Testament Commentaries*, vol. 8, *Romans and Thessalonians* (Grand Rapids, MI:
Eerdmans, 1991), 85.

and by accounting and accepting their persons as righteous; not for any thing wrought in them, or done by them, but for Christ's sake alone; nor by imputing faith itself, the act of believing, or any other evangelical obedience to them, as their righteousness; but by imputing the obedience and satisfaction of Christ unto them, they receiving and resting on Him and His righteousness by faith; which faith they have not of themselves, it is the gift of God.[24]

The same definition is very clear here. We get a sense of how Edwards was later attempting to defend, creatively rearticulate, and communicate with different language his doctrine of justification by the number of terms in this definition that Edwards picks up and discusses: "infusing" (though he uses the word in a different sense from here, for he is not talking about "infusing righteousness"), "evangelical obedience" (which he discusses in the sense of obedience that comes from faith, not an obedience that gives justification), and faith as the "instrument" of justification, a term found later in the Confession (Edwards does not like this term because he thinks it is open to misunderstanding). Still, when you read the Westminster Confession and then read Edwards you can see why some people's alarm bells ring.

If I were to attempt to define justification according to the Reformation Protestant canon, I would say something like this: "To be justified is to be declared right (or 'just') by God on the basis of Christ crucified. Christ removes our sin and credits us his righteousness. We can receive this free gift of justification through faith alone, not because we have done anything to deserve it. Faith is the work of God's Holy Spirit in our lives. Those who truly believe live as a result a new life following Christ."

Such a statement would have been de rigueur and basic for New England Puritanism. For evidence, take John Cotton's *Milk for Babes*, a basic catechism included with the *New England Primer* (the tool for teaching children their alphabet):

---

[24] Westminster Confession of Faith, "Of Justification," 11.1.

> *Qu.* How doth the spirit of grace apply Christ, and his promise of grace unto you, and keepe you in him?

> *Answ.* By begetting in me faith to receive him: Prayer to call upon him: Repentence to mourne after him: and new obedience to serve him.[25]

That's the basic, bottom-line Reformation Protestant assumption about justification held by New England Puritans like Edwards. All of his sophisticated articulation and discussion takes as its starting point this "milk."

How Edwards's View of Justification Addresses Some Contemporary Questions about Justification

George Hunsinger says, "Those dissatisfied with the arguments of scholars like E. P. Sanders and James Dunn will find a welcome ally in Edwards, should they choose to consult him."[26] Whether or not Edwards is a "welcome ally" depends, as Hunsinger points out, on your level of satisfaction with some of the contemporary arguments. More to the point, however, Edwards's formulation asks some searching questions of these modern attempts at a new kind of justification theory, which friend and foe alike need to consider.

For instance, take the often overlooked opening foray of Edwards's *Justification by Faith Alone* lectures. First, Romans 4:5 cannot mean that godliness is any form of ground for justification, or that godliness is antecedent to justification, for:

> Which words can't imply less than that God in the act of justification, has no regard to anything in the person justified, as godliness, or any goodness in him; but that nextly, or immediately before this act, God beholds him only as an ungodly or wicked creature; so that godliness in the person to be justified is not so

---

[25] John Cotton, "Milk for Babes. Drawn Out of the Breasts of Both Testaments. Chiefly, for the Spirituall Nourishment of Boston Babes in Either England: But May Be of Like Use for Any Children (1646)," ed. Paul Royster (1646). Electronic Texts in American Studies, Libraries at University of Nebraska-Lincoln, Digital Commons, Paper 18, http://digitalcommons.unl.edu/cgi/viewcontent.cgi?article=1018&context=etas.

[26] Hunsinger, "Dispositional Soteriology," 107.

antecedent to his justification as to be the ground of it. When it is said that God justifies the ungodly, 'tis as absurd to suppose that our godliness, taken as some goodness in us, is the ground of our justification, as when it is said that Christ gave sight to the blind, to suppose that sight was prior to, and the ground of that act of mercy in Christ, or as if it should be said that such an one by his bounty has made a poor man rich, to suppose that it was the wealth of this poor man that was the ground of this bounty towards him, and was the price by which it was procured.[27]

So thinking that Romans 4:5 means that justification is grounded in some form of personal godliness is as "absurd" (Edwards's word) as saying that Christ gave sight to the blind on the basis of the sight of the blind person, or that the seeing was previous to the blind person's seeing. This is because God is justifying the *ungodly*, as Edwards says.

Second, the words "works" and "ungodly" exclude the possibility that Paul is speaking about the ceremonial law, because:

It appears that by "him that worketh not" in this verse, is not meant only one that don't conform to the ceremonial law, because "he that worketh not," and "the ungodly" are evidently synonymous expressions, or what signify the same; it appears by the manner of their connection; if it ben't so, to what purpose is the latter expression "the ungodly" brought in? The context gives no other occasion for it, but only to show that the grace of the gospel appears in that God in justification has no regard to any godliness of ours: the foregoing verse is, "Now to him that worketh is the reward not reckoned of grace, but of debt": in that verse 'tis evident, that gospel grace consists in the rewards being given without works; and in this verse which nextly follows it and in sense is connected with it, 'tis evident that gospel grace consists in a man's being justified that is "ungodly"; by which it is most plain that by "him that worketh not," and him that is "ungodly," are meant the same thing; and that therefore not only works of the ceremonial law are excluded in this business of justification, but works of morality and godliness.[28]

---

[27] *The Works of Jonathan Edwards*, vol. 1, ed. Edward Hickman (Carlisle, PA: Banner of Truth, 1834), 622.
[28] Ibid.

Because in the biblical context "works not" and "ungodliness" mean the same thing in the argument, the law that justification happens without cannot merely be the law of ceremony, but must be the law of all works of morality and godliness.

Lastly, the example of David, which Paul mentions subsequent to the key text (Rom. 4:6–8), shows that it is works most generally that Paul is talking about, not the ceremonial law:

> How are these words of David to the Apostle's purpose? Or how do they prove any such thing, as that righteousness is imputed without works, unless it be because the word imputed is used and the subject of the imputation is mentioned, as a sinner, and consequently destitute of a moral righteousness? For David says no such thing, as that he is forgiven without the works of the ceremonial law; there is no hint of the ceremonial law, or reference to it, in the words.[29]

Because David performed the works of the ceremonial law as a pious Old Testament king, there is no possibility that the works he is referring to are anything other than moral works, and that therefore he is a sinner (despite his ceremonial obedience)[30] who needs justifying.

I am sure that others have noted that Romans 4:5 and its context is a crux of the debate involving James Dunn and other "new perspective" scholars, but long before them, Edwards points out that case with razor-sharp exactitude (as well as a certain lack of modern politically correct finesse: "absurd," "it is most plain," etc.). Of course Sanders's groundbreaking work was not available to him as evidence, but no one—surely—really thinks that the essential argument that the "law" in Paul is merely ceremonial is "new." That's what Jerome believed, and Chrysostom did not; it's what Luther was arguing against in his commentary on Galatians. It's a debate that, if not quite as old as the hills, is certainly as old as Jerome and Chrysostom. As far as that is the central issue, Edwards's arguments need to continue to be considered.

---

[29] *WJE Online*, vol. 19.
[30] Edwards's point is similar to the one that Gathercole has made about this passage.

But more generally than the specifics of exegesis of key texts in the contemporary debate, Edwards has significant responses to the classic questions posed to the doctrine of justification by faith alone. He identifies six objections: (1) there are promises of eternal life in the Bible given to our own virtue; (2) our holiness is necessary to be ready for heaven, and therefore really what God accepts; (3) the Bible talks of eternal rewards given for good deeds; (4) the Bible talks of a moral worthiness being the basis for getting Christ; (5) repentance is described as that which gives justification; and (6) the James 2:21–24 objection ("by works a man is justified, and not by faith only").

Of those six objections five seem to be subdivisions of the same basic objection, namely that in various places, the Bible appears to ascribe eternal reward on the basis of our good deeds. And the sixth objection is a particularly well-known example of that same phenomenon. Basically, the objection to justification by faith alone is that the Bible seems to some to teach something other than justification by faith alone. How successful Edwards is in defeating these objections is up for grabs.

What is especially noteworthy, however, is that the precise form of Edwards's doctrine of justification by faith alone allows itself to be particularly immune to the objections. This is where all the discussion about "infusion" and "evangelical obedience" and the like comes from. Edwards is insisting that because a real transition takes place, those who believe are justified, changed, and regenerated, and therefore (in the classic old Puritan way of expressing it) our works are a sign of Christ's work in us, and it is Christ in us who is rewarded. The believer's union with Christ is right at the heart of Edwards's defense—as it is in most successful defenses of the doctrine: "I am crucified with Christ: nevertheless I live; yet not I, but Christ liveth in me" (Gal. 2:20).

Conclusion

Edwards has some particular contributions to make to the theological discussion about justification. He emphasizes fairly strongly the "union with Christ" motif, which is not that atypical, but he does so in ways that have a specific "Edwardsean" flavor. The virtues have a "concatenation" together. There is an "infusion" of something real, a "sanctification" in the soul. Faith, hope, and love are names that are interchangeably used for a common phenomenon in Scripture, a disposition (this use of "disposition" goes back to Edwards's long discussions elsewhere about "the sense of the heart," and his whole soul psychology, as he seeks to counter Enlightenment rationalization[31]).

We find within Edwards a certain engagement with the preparationist scheme of salvation, which he emphasizes as being particularly gracious, and yet sticks with, in the main, to the disagreement of many of his later interpreters. He also seeks to counter the "Arminian" (in his sense) critique of justification by faith alone that it left too little room for works, and the deist critique that it was too nonsensically mystical, in such a way that at times his doctrine veers close to the shoals he is trying to avoid.

But, to say that Edwards's doctrine of justification is nearly Roman Catholic is, to use an Edwardsean impoliteness, "absurd." Let him speak for himself: "We are justified only by faith in Christ, and not by any manner of virtue or goodness of our own."[32]

---

[31] Moody, *Jonathan Edwards and the Enlightenment*, 61–65.
[32] *WJE Online*, vol. 19.

CHAPTER TWO

By Word and Spirit: Jonathan Edwards on Redemption, Justification, and Regeneration

Kyle Strobel

This chapter addresses the theological contours of Edwards's doctrine of justification, with a specific eye to redemption, imputation, and regeneration. The overall aim is to highlight the interconnection of Edwards's theology of redemption. Doing so necessitates focused attention on God's economic activity as Word and Spirit as the controlling mechanism of redemption. In short, we argue that Edwards's development of soteriological loci occurs *under* his analysis of the person and work of Christ and the nature and gift of the Spirit. Like all good Reformed accounts, Edwards's doctrine of justification focuses primarily on *God's movement* in Word and Spirit to redeem fallen humanity. To appropriately analyze Edwards's doctrine of justification, one must align it with the specific contours of redemption as movements of *this* Word and *this* Spirit, themselves grounded only within the eternal, immanent life of God. As noted by John Webster, "Soteriology is a derivative doctrine, and no derivative doctrine may occupy the material place which is properly reserved for the Christian doctrine of God, from which alone all other doctrines derive."[1] Edwards is an ideal example of this axiom. What follows, therefore, is an account of redemption that

---

[1] John Webster, "'It Was the Will of the Lord to Bruise Him': Soteriology and the Doctrine of God," in *God of Salvation: Soteriology in Theological Perspective* (Surrey, UK: Ashgate, 2011), 16.

is primarily focused on the persons of God in the economy, and left aside is the detailed background development of God's life *in se* and the *pactum salutis*. Nevertheless, it should be clear that these doctrines serve as the ground and schematic upon which Edwards constructs his soteriology.

In brief, Edwards's doctrine of redemption answers the problem raised in his account of the fall. In the fall, humankind lost not only an innocent standing before God, but also the Holy Spirit of God that had been infused into them as a holy *super*natural principle of life.[2] For fallen humanity to be redeemed, it needs to be declared righteous—that is, to secure a righteousness that includes both remission of sin as well as a positive righteousness imputed—and needs to have holiness (the *Holy* Spirit) infused as a new principle. For Edwards, Christ's life, from incarnation to resurrection, is the culminating work of God to address this lack in sinful humanity. What Edwards posits is a Trinitarian movement to redeem based on the idea of "purchase."

The Purchase of God

By grounding the questions and concerns of justification in the overarching movement of God in Word and Spirit to redeem, we start with the *purchase* that God has made. In Edwards's words, "The Holy Spirit is the great purchase of Christ. God the Father is the person of whom the purchase is made; God the Son is the person who makes the purchase, and the Holy Spirit is the gift purchased."[3] Prior to the incarnation, nothing had been done to "purchase" redemption, and "as soon as Christ was incarnate, then the purchase began immediately without delay"; similarly, "nothing was done after his resurrection to purchase redemption for men."[4] This does not mean the ascension is meaningless for redemption, but rather, it is the event "whereby believers are made

---

[2] See Jonathan Edwards, *The Works of Jonathan Edwards* (hereafter WJE), vol. 3, *Original Sin*, ed. Clyde A. Holbrook (New Haven, CT: Yale University Press, 1970), 381–83.

[3] Jonathan Edwards, "Charity and Its Fruits," in *WJE*, vol. 8, *Ethical Writings*, ed. Paul Ramsay (New Haven, CT: Yale University Press, 1989), 353.

[4] Jonathan Edwards, "A History of the Work of Redemption," in *WJE*, vol. 9, *A History of the Work of Redemption*, ed. John F. Wilson (New Haven, CT: Yale University Press, 1989), 295.

partakers of the benefits of Christ's righteousness."[5] Edwards goes on to compare the ascension to the high priest going into the holiest of holies, but now as the priest *and* sacrifice.

The work of redemption is a Trinitarian work, where the Son purchases the Spirit from the Father for the elect. "What Christ does for men in the office of a mediator between God and men is to procure the Holy Ghost for man and bestow it upon him, *and the whole may be summed up in that.*"[6] Jesus's mediatorial role is more than just standing in a gap between two opposing parties; he reconciles those parties in his person. "[I]nasmuch as he was a divine person, he brought down divinity with him to us. So he brought God down to man, and then he ascended to God. Inasmuch as he was in the human nature, he carried up humanity with him to God."[7] Christ as mediator intercedes for his people, as truly one of them, bringing his sacrifice, *himself*, before the Father. Therefore, in Christ's person, redemption is accomplished in full. Christ, the head of the church, is judged, justified, and glorified as the second Adam, the Adam in whom all believers find forgiveness, mercy, and life. Christ, as a federal head, does not simply act for his own sake, but to purchase salvation through his obedience for the elect. It is by being in this new "Adam" that believers are saved, and it is through the purchase made on their behalf that they are found to be truly *in* him.

By focusing on the economic activity of the persons of the triune God, that is, by orienting redemption around the purchase of the *Spirit* by *Christ* from the *Father*, Edwards emphasizes God's *self-giving* rather than the idea that God only gives certain benefits. A proper grammar of redemption arises from attending to the acts of Word and Spirit, rather than any benefits procured by Word and Spirit. In other words, redemption broadly, and justification specifically, is oriented by the Son's unwavering love for the saints,

---

[5] Jonathan Edwards, "The Threefold Work of the Holy Ghost," in *WJE*, vol. 14, *Sermons and Discourses 1723–1729*, ed. Kenneth P. Minkema (New Haven, CT: Yale University Press, 1997), 392.
[6] Jonathan Edwards, "Jesus Christ Is the Great Mediator and Head of Union," in *The Blessing of God: Previously Unpublished Sermons of Jonathan Edwards*, ed. Michael D. McMullen (Nashville: Broadman & Holman, 2003), 316 (emphasis added).
[7] Ibid., 322–23.

a love that drives the work of redemption and, ultimately, unites believers to Christ's own life.[8]

By purchasing the Spirit for the elect, Christ purchases communion and participation in the very life of God. This participation is not mediated in a metaphysical register, as if humanity were somehow to merge into the essence of God, but is fundamentally a relational notion (upholding persons as such).[9] It is in this sense that Edwards can say, "We shall in a sort be partakers of his [Christ's] relation to the Father or his communion with him in his Sonship. We shall not only be the sons of God by regeneration but a kind of participation of the Sonship of the eternal Son."[10] This relational participation with God is given through the Spirit, the bond of love by which God communes with creatures.[11] The relational character of communion and participation is most fully expressed through his use of marital and familial imagery, such as:

---

[8] Edwards states, somewhat provocatively, that "by the incarnation [God] is really become passionate to his own, so that he loves them with such a sort of love as we have. . . . Now this passionate love of Christ, by virtue of the union with the divine nature, is in a sort infinite," Jonathan Edwards, "The 'Miscellanies,' no. z," in *WJE*, vol. 13, *The "Miscellanies," a–z, aa–zz, 1–500*, ed. Thomas A. Schafer (New Haven, CT: Yale University Press, 1994), 176–77. Furthermore, "Everything that was contrived and done for the redemption and salvation of believers, and every benefit they have by it, is wholly and perfectly from the free, eternal, distinguishing love and infinite grace of Christ towards them," Jonathan Edwards, *WJE*, vol. 24, *The Blank Bible*, ed. Stephen Stein (New Haven, CT: Yale University Press, 2006), 617. In "Miscellanies," nos. 1352 and 1360, Edwards illustrates the imputation of righteousness by focusing *on the relations* inherent in the discussion—the perfect Father, Jesus as the patron of the elect, and the elect themselves. I summarize here: For Edwards, Jesus, as the elect's patron, based on his union of nature and love with the Father, has, through his nature and love to the elect, united himself fully to them, taking on their cause as his own, and suffering all that needed to be suffered for their full redemption. The role of the client, simply enough, is to be a client, to cleave to and put his trust in Christ, that Christ, his patron, will do all that is needed in recommending him to the Father. See Jonathan Edwards, "The 'Miscellanies,' nos. 1352 and 1360," in *WJE*, vol. 23, *The "Miscellanies," 1153–1360*, ed. Douglas A. Sweeney (New Haven, CT: Yale University Press, 2004), 481–92, 713–16.

[9] "The soul is espoused and married unto Jesus Christ; the believing soul is the bride and spouse of the Son of God." "The 'Miscellanies,' no. 37," *WJE*, 13:219.

[10] Jonathan Edwards, "Thy Name Is as Ointment Poured Forth," in *The Blessing of God*, 177.

[11] See Jonathan Edwards, "Discourse on the Trinity," in *WJE*, vol. 21, *Writings on the Trinity, Grace and Faith*, ed. Sang Hyun Lee (New Haven, CT: Yale University Press, 2003), 122, 129. "The communion of saints with Christ does certainly very much consist in that receiving of his fullness and partaking of his grace, spoken of, John 1:16, 'Of his fullness have we all received, and grace for grace'; and in partaking of that Spirit which God gives not by measure unto him. Partaking of Christ's holiness and grace, his nature, inclinations, tendencies, love and desires, comforts and delights, must be to have communion with Christ. Yea, a believer's communion with the Father and the Son does mainly consist in his partaking of the Holy Ghost, as appears by II Cor. 13:14, 'The grace of the Lord Jesus Christ, and the love of God, and the *communion* of the Holy Ghost,'" "Treatise on Grace," *WJE*, 21:158.

This was the design of Christ, to bring it to pass, that he, and his Father, and his people, might all be united in one . . . that those that the Father has given him, should be brought into the household of God; that he, and his Father, and his people, should be as it were one society, one family; that the church should be as it were admitted into the society of the blessed Trinity.[12]

Therefore, in order to understand justification within the broader scope of redemption, Edwards's depiction of pneumatological union and participation with Christ must be understood as the doctrinal moorings within which to consider the discrete doctrines of imputation and regeneration. Or, to retain our primary focus, we must locate imputation and regeneration in the work of the Son and Spirit in the economy.

Justification and Imputation

When justification is understood under the purchase of the Spirit by Christ, then the "thinness" of Edwards's doctrine of justification becomes clear.[13] Justification is "thin" in the sense that it does not cover much theological ground, or—to continue the spatial metaphor—it does not take up much doctrinal space. This thinness, it is important to emphasize, does not in any way degrade the importance or centrality of the doctrine. Far from it. We can understand the doctrine of justification to be like a hinge on a

---

[12] Jonathan Edwards, "The Excellency of Christ," in *WJE*, vol. 19, *Sermons and Discourses 1734–1738*, ed. M. X. Lesser (New Haven, CT: Yale University Press, 2001), 593.

[13] The downfall in much of the secondary literature is a failure to recognize the "thinness" of justification. McDermott, for instance, claims that, for Edwards, "justification changes the soul," Gerald McDermott, "Jonathan Edwards on Justification by Faith—More Protestant or Catholic?" *Pro Ecclesia* 27/1 (Winter 2008): 106. Schafer, taking the opposite stance, claims that Edwards tended to "bypass" justification in favor of virtue, Thomas A. Schafer, "Jonathan Edwards and Justification by Faith," *Church History* 20/4 (Dec. 1951): 62. Chamberlain notes that justification ceased to be the "central organizing concept of his soteriology," and seems to assume a rather odd picture of soteriology. Regardless of emphasis or "dogmatic space," the doctrine of justification is the hinge on which all true religion turns for Edwards, regardless of early or late material, or his emphasis upon grace, infusion, or sanctification. See *WJE*, vol. 18, *The "Miscellanies" 501–832*, ed. Ava Chamberlain (New Haven, CT: Yale University Press, 2000), 38. Waddington, helpfully, notes that Schafer and Chamberlain, as representative examples of much of the secondary literature, collapses the forensic (justification) with the transformational (regeneration/sanctification), Jeffrey C. Waddington, "Jonathan Edwards's 'Ambiguous and Somewhat Precarious' Doctrine of Justification," *Westminster Theological Journal* 66 (2004): 359, see also 359–60 fn8. McClymond falters at this point as well, Michael J. McClymond, "Salvation as Divinization: Jonathan Edwards, Gregory Palamas and the Theological Uses of Neoplatonism," in *Jonathan Edwards: Philosophical Theologian*, eds. Paul Helm and Oliver Crisp (Aldershot, UK: Ashgate, 2003), 140.

door. A hinge is small (thin), in that it has little mass in comparison with the door itself, but without the hinge the door is simply a wall. In fact, the entire identity of a door is established by the hinge.[14] Justification orders redemption by orienting soteriological loci as well as the economic activity of the Son. As we have emphasized, the real center of redemption, with all its facets, is the economic movement of Word and Spirit. The doctrine of justification establishes the work that the Son must do to truly redeem and the necessary corollaries of this work in the elect. Michael Horton observes that this era of Protestant orthodoxy, as a result of the polemical environment, "walled off" justification from any sort of inward change, thereby bifurcating the discussion into forensic justification on one hand and transformation on the other.[15] Therefore, like others in his day, Edwards narrows his doctrine of justification to focus solely on how it is God can (and does) declare fallen humanity righteous.

In 1738 Edwards published a book entitled *Discourses on Various Important Subjects*, including a reworked lecture on justification which remained, throughout his life, his most detailed and focused exposition of the doctrine (hereafter *Justification by Faith*). He begins the work with four important qualifications. First, God's declaration of righteousness is only upon the ungodly.[16] Second, God declares the ungodly righteous not because of works of any kind: "ungodly" and "him that worketh not" are synonymous terms. This work (or lack thereof) is not only limited to the ceremonial law, but includes all works of morality and

---

[14] Calvin talks about justification as the "hinge" upon which religion turns, which is an interesting parallel to what I am highlighting. John Calvin, *Institutes of the Christian Religion*, ed. John T. McNeill, trans. Ford Lewis Battles, 2 vols. (Louisville, KY: Westminster John Knox, 1960), 3.xi.1.
[15] Michael S. Horton, *Covenant and Salvation: Union with Christ* (Louisville, KY: Westminster John Knox Press, 2007), 198. Edwards's distinctive attempt to collapse this "wall" is to emphasize Word and Spirit on the front end of the discussion and then focus the latter end on the inherent relation of perseverance to faith itself. Notably, the opposition, in part, denied supernatural illumination, infused grace, and justification by faith alone. We should not be surprised to find all three emphasized in Edwards's account. "Freedom of the Will," in *WJE*, vol. 1, *Freedom of the Will*, ed. Paul Ramsay (New Haven, CT: Yale University Press, 1957), 374. See also *Original Sin*, *WJE*, 3:319–26 for more polemical engagement on justification.
[16] There is some discussion whether Edwards can truly see his position as justification of the *ungodly*. See McDermott, "Jonathan Edwards on Justification by Faith," 103; McClymond, "Salvation as Divinization," 140; and Conrad Cherry, *The Theology of Jonathan Edwards: A Reappraisal* (Bloomington, IN: Indiana University Press, 1966), 96–106.

godliness. Third, when Scripture talks about having faith rather than works, faith is not a species of work or a "course of obedience" in its own right. Fourth, God declares people without any righteousness of their own to be righteous. This righteousness is "counted" or "imputed" to the believer and is not his or her own.[17] These four points mark the contours of Edwards's account of justification and are the building blocks he uses to develop his doctrine: "*We are justified only by faith in Christ, and not by any manner of virtue or goodness of our own.*"[18]

Justification denotes our being approved as free from guilt and its deserved punishment, as well as having received "righteousness belonging to him that entitles to the reward of life."[19] The judge accepts a person as having both a "negative righteousness" (pardon of sin) and a positive righteousness, and therefore accepts her as truly righteous (rather than merely free from guilt). Justification, in other words, is not placing the believer in the same place as Adam was prior to the fall. Adam's innocence, as should be obvious, was not enough; the righteousness believers need includes both innocence *and* obedience. For believers to receive *only* innocence would fail to truly justify them. Edwards explains that *Christ's* righteousness is accepted for us in place of the *inherent* righteousness we ought to have in ourselves.[20] His concern is to show that Christ's perfect obedience is "reckoned to our account," as though we had "performed it ourselves."[21] Justification has to take into consideration the broader work of Christ, so that believers are put in a different place than Adam was originally, namely, without guilt. Edwards summarizes by saying, "So on the same account we han't eternal life merely on the account of being void of guilt (as Adam was at first existence), which we have by the

---

[17] "Justification by Faith Alone," *WJE*, 19:147–49. Michael McClenahan notes that, "For Edwards these are the main areas of contention between the Reformed and the Arminians: the status before God of sinful man; the absence of works from justification; the role of saving faith; and the imputation of righteousness." Michael McClenahan, "Jonathan Edwards' Doctrine of Justification in the Period up to the First Great Awakening" (PhD diss., University of Oxford, 2006), 152.
[18] "Justification by Faith Alone," *WJE*, 19:149.
[19] Ibid., 150.
[20] Ibid., 186.
[21] Ibid.

atonement of Christ; but on the account of Christ's activeness in obedience, and doing well."[22] Edwards continues:

> God doth in the sentence of justification pronounce a man per-fectly righteous, or else he would need a further justification after he is justified: his sins being removed by Christ's atone-ment, is not sufficient for his justification; for justifying a man, as has already been shown, is not merely pronouncing him inno-cent or without guilt, but standing right, with regard to the rule that he is under, and righteous unto life; but this, according to the established rule of nature, reason, and divine appointment, is a positive perfect righteousness.[23]

Edwards cannot be charged with lacking a forensic focus, but he also cannot be said to propose merely a "legal fiction."[24] He claims that "God neither will nor can justify a person without a righteousness . . . if a person should be justified without a righ-teousness, the judgment would not be according to truth," claim-ing that "the sentence of justification would be a false sentence, unless there be a righteousness performed that is by the judge properly looked upon as his."[25] For Edwards, justification is *truly* legal, therefore, according to law, and the pronouncement of jus-tification is "judicial," the act of a judge. There is no working around that fact. In order for the judge to be honorable and righ-teous, another righteousness must be looked upon as the sinner's own. In Edwards's words, "The judge's work is two-fold: it is to determine first what is fact, and then whether what is in fact be

---

[22] Ibid., 187. The implication is that the Arminian view does not actually deal with justifica-tion per se, but only addresses the issues inherent to the atonement. Michael McClenahan, in my mind, correctly outlines Edwards's polemic against the "Arminians" as against Anglican theologians in general and Archbishop of Canterbury John Tillotson in particular. McClenahan, "Jonathan Edwards' Doctrine of Justification," 49–147.

[23] "Justification by Faith Alone," *WJE*, 19:190–91.

[24] John Owen lays out the claim often leveled against the Reformed position: "The righteousness itself being, as they [opponents] phrase it, *putative, imaginary,* a *chimera,* a *fiction,* it can have no real accidents—nothing that can be really predicated concerning it." Owen, *Faith and Its Evidences,* 17 vols., *The Works of John Owen,* vol. 5 (London: Banner of Truth, 1965), 112. Furthermore, Edwards, in claiming that the declaration of righteousness depends upon a real foundation, seems to be following Owen who states, "It is not a *naked pronunciation* or declaration of any one to be righ-teous, without a just and sufficient foundation for the judgment of God declared therein. God declares no man to be righteous but him who is so; the whole question being how he comes so to be." Ibid., 173.

[25] "Justification by Faith Alone," *WJE*, 19:188.

according to rule, or according to the law."[26] Edwards establishes this true declaration with two important dogmatic moves: first, Christ is justified by the Father through his act of obedience, suffering, and death under the law, and second, that justification is only available by being united to Christ.

Christ had entered into the *pactum salutis* with the Father before time began, and therefore, prior to creation, had "virtually" stood in the place of humanity.[27] Once Christ took on human nature he was under the law, and because of that law and the guilt of humanity upon him, he "could not be acquitted, till he had suffered, nor rewarded till he had obeyed."[28] When Christ is raised from the dead, therefore, he is raised as the justified One, which entails both acquittance from guilt *and* acceptance of glory for his obedience.[29] In faith, believers "partake with Christ in this his justification," not only in being found innocent by the judge, but in accepting *his* reward for themselves.[30]

By making Christ the justified One, in whom justification itself resides, Edwards depicts Christ as the centerpiece of redemption. By focusing on union as the means by which justification is obtained, he portrays the Spirit alongside him. Emphasizing the centrality of God's economy in redemption, Edwards narrates justification through participation. Adam's failure is taken up by Christ, who Edwards calls "our second surety." In *Christ's* "justification all who believe in him, and whose surety he is, are virtually justified."[31] God the Father justifies Christ by raising him from the dead, and, Edwards continues to emphasize, "the justification of a believer *is not other* than his being admitted to communion in, or participation of the justification of this head

---

[26] Ibid., 190.

[27] Ibid., 192.

[28] Ibid., 191.

[29] Ibid.

[30] Ibid.

[31] Ibid. Later in his work on justification Edwards states, "Hence (by the way), the love, honor, and obedience of Christ towards God, has infinite value, from the excellency and dignity of the person in whom these qualifications were inherent: and the reason why we needed a person of infinite dignity to obey for us, was because of our infinite comparative meanness, who had disobeyed, whereby our disobedience was infinitely aggravated: we needed one, the worthiness of whose obedience, might be answerable to the unworthiness of our disobedience; and therefore needed one who was as great and worthy, as we were unworthy." Ibid., 162.

and surety of all believers."[32] Christ's role as mediator and federal head involves not only his obedience, but also his justification. Christ does not procure a treasure and then hand it out to those with faith; *Christ* and the *Spirit* are the treasure. The Spirit is given to unite to Christ, where righteousness, redemption, and justification reside. Speaking of redemption, in other words, is not primarily talk about justification, as important as that is, but is first and foremost a discussion of participation in Christ through his Spirit.

Faith and Union

Such concentration upon Christ alone brings all the emphasis on faith alone—*solus Christus* demands *sola fide*. In other words, justification is by faith *because* it is in Christ. This leads naturally to Edwards's question: "How this is said to be by faith alone, without any manner of virtue or goodness of our own?"[33] How does faith, a virtue, not concern the merit and holiness *inherent* in the believer, when faith, in fact, is a part of a believer's inherent holiness?[34] Edwards answers by denying that faith is accepted because of its goodness or excellency. Rather, it is accepted as meet and suitable "purely from the relation faith has to the person in whom this benefit is to be had, *or as it unites to that Mediator*, in and by whom we are justified."[35] Faith is a mode of relation and union whose *telos* is not justification, *but Christ*. It is not a moral quality,

---

[32] Ibid., 151 (emphasis added). Hunsinger argues that Edwards undermines Calvin's notion that believers participate in Christ's righteousness only through fellowship with his person. George Hunsinger, "Dispositional Soteriology: Jonathan Edwards on Justification by Faith Alone," *Westminster Theological Journal* 66 (2004): 112. This seems to me a rather odd claim since that is the main thrust of Edwards's "Justification by Faith." Hunsinger's concern stems from Edwards's focus on perseverance, which is beyond the bounds of our discussion here. Hunsinger, while providing a lucid and erudite critique of Edwards's doctrine, seems to allow the second half of the "Justification by Faith" material to reinterpret (or, if nothing else, choke out) the first half, where Edwards makes his primary argument, which we are analyzing here.

[33] Ibid., 154.

[34] Ibid.

[35] Ibid., 155 (emphasis added). Later in the work Edwards delineates *moral* and *natural* fitness. In justification, faith is seen as a natural fitness, where it is meet and suitable for the believer to be seen as one with Christ, and not a moral fitness, where faith is taken as a virtue (excellent in itself). He claims that "there is nothing that is accepted as any godliness or excellency of the person, till after justification . . . the acceptance even of faith as any goodness or loveliness of the believer, follows justification: the goodness is on the forementioned account justly looked upon as nothing, until the man is justified: and therefore the man is respected in justification, as in himself altogether hateful." Ibid., 164–65.

but a relational one. Jesus Christ has been justified, and therefore the central question for the doctrine of justification is how fallen, broken, and depraved humanity can be understood to be *in* Christ, as one with him, when they have nothing to offer.

Rather than opting for a declaration from God that makes the sinner righteous in justification, Edwards addresses both faith *in* and union *with* Christ as the reality which makes the declaration of righteousness true. Edwards offers three clarifications regarding this union. First, in Scripture this union and relation is represented with metaphors of membership in Christ, using images of the head, branches to the trunk, and marriage between a husband and wife.[36] Second, Scripture states that it is the reality of Christians "in Christ" that provides the "ground of their right to his benefits."[37] The twofold movement in justification therefore is being *in him* and then being *made righteous*, or, in other words, "[o]ur being in him is the ground of our being accepted."[38] As regards these various metaphors, Edwards argues that "they are looked upon . . . as one in law: so there is a *legal* union between Christ and true Christians; so that . . . one, in some respects, is accepted for the other, by the Supreme Judge."[39]

Edwards's third clarification highlights faith as that which qualifies a believer so that "in the sight of God . . . he should be looked upon as having Christ's satisfaction and righteousness belonging to him."[40] Therefore, it is by being in Christ that the believer has Christ's benefits and merits. Edwards again focuses the discussion on the person of Christ himself:

> 'Tis easy to see how our having Christ's merits and benefits belonging to us, follows from our having (if I may so speak) Christ himself belonging to us, or a being united to him; and if so it must also be easy to see how, or in what manner, that, in a person, that on his part makes up the union between his soul and

---

[36] Ibid., 155.
[37] Ibid., 156.
[38] Ibid. The distinction between being *in him* with being *made righteous* is a logical rather than temporal one.
[39] Ibid. (emphasis added).
[40] Ibid.

Christ, should be the thing on the account of which God looks
on it meet that he should have Christ's merits belonging to him.[41]

Faith, as Edwards suggests here, is a quality in a believer that
is not seen as moral or valuable in its own right, but is looked
upon by God as "meet" for Christ's benefits to belong to him/her.
This is how Edwards parses the idea of justification by faith. It is
by faith in that faith is the necessary manner (one could say condition) by which one *receives Christ*, and being united with Christ
is seen as a "meet" and "fit" qualification for receiving Christ's
benefits.[42] Justification, therefore, as a legal declaration, follows
upon the act of union, whereby believers become *legally* one with
Christ, and are therefore suitable participants of his benefits.

Edwards is adamant about the distinction he has drawn
between faith as suitable for legal union and faith as a virtue,
and asserts again that, "God don't give those that believe, an
union with, or an interest in the Savior, *in reward for faith*, but only
because faith is the soul's active uniting with Christ, or is itself the
very act of unition, on their part."[43] There is an important role for
the individual in faith, but it is not a *moral* role. Edwards provides
some helpful clarification of his position:

> God in requiring this in order to an union with Christ as one
> of his people, treats men as reasonable creatures, capable of act,
> and choice; and hence sees it fit that they only, that are one with
> Christ by their own act, *should be looked upon as one in law*: what is
> real in the union between Christ and his people, is the founda-
> tion of what is legal; that is, it is something really in them, and
> between them, uniting them, that is the ground of the suitable-
> ness of their being accounted as one by the Judge: and if there
> is any act, or qualification in believers, that is of that uniting

[41] Ibid.
[42] Thomas Goodwin's work, *The Object and Acts of Justifying Faith*, comes to mind here, when he
states, "We are not made righteous by the act of believing; no, we are constituted and made
righteous by that obedience of Christ on which we believe." The act of believing does nothing to
achieve righteousness, but only unites to Christ. Thomas Goodwin, "The Object and Acts of Justifying Faith," in *The Works of Thomas Goodwin* (London: James Nichol, 1864), 8:289. Furthermore,
Goodwin claims, "Marrying a man's daughter . . . is not a condition, but an essential ingredient
into the constitutive nature of the thing, and the means of enjoying her person." Ibid., 252.
Edwards is less concerned with the term "condition," but their worries are the same.
[43] "Justification by Faith Alone," *WJE*, 19:158 (emphasis added).

nature, that it is meet on that account that the Judge should look upon 'em, and accept 'em as one.[44]

Note first that in the declaration of justification, God treats human persons as *rational* creatures. God does not, therefore, bypass the faculties of humanity, but respects his created design. Second, justification functions in a legal register answering legal questions, and Edwards grounds the legal declaration of justification in union with Christ. Union answers the question of how Christ's righteousness can be accepted by the Father as the believer's own; in other words, union makes imputation possible. In union Christ and believers are "one in law," in a similar fashion, I suggest, as husband and wife. Faith justifies, Edwards asserts, "as it thus makes Christ and the believer one in the acceptance of the Supreme Judge."[45] It is in this vein that Edwards states,

> When a man offers himself to a woman in marriage, he don't give himself to her as a reward of her receiving him in marriage: her receiving him is not considered as a worthy deed in her, for which he rewards her, by giving himself to her; but 'tis by her receiving him, that the union is made, by which she hath him for her husband: 'tis on her part the unition itself.[46]

Believers come to have a true relation to God, in Christ, by the Spirit who is sent to indwell their hearts, and, as we see below, to unite them to Christ, illuminate Christ for them, and act in their persons as a vital principle of holiness. Union, again, it must be stressed, does not function in a metaphysical register, but a relational one.[47] This is what Edwards surely means when he states, "Our communion with God the Father and God the Son consists in our partaking of the Holy Ghost, which is their Spirit: for to

---

[44] Ibid. (emphasis added).
[45] Ibid.
[46] Ibid., 201
[47] Edwards states, "There is a union with Christ, by the indwelling of the love of Christ, two ways: first, as 'tis from Christ, and is the very Spirit and life and fullness of Christ; and second, as it acts to Christ: for the very nature of it is love and union of heart to him." Ibid., 195. In his "Notebook on Faith," Edwards shows concerns with metaphysical terms to describe faith such as "embrace" or "adhere to," which are later replaced with the language of "closing." "Notebook on Faith," *WJE*, 21:433.

have communion or fellowship with another, is to partake with them of their good in their fullness, in union and society with them."[48] The common good shared with God is his Spirit. "To partake of the Holy Ghost is to have that love of the Father and the grace of the Son."[49] This union does not undermine the creature *qua* creature, but instead upholds it in the relation they were created to partake in. Union is relational communion in a society of united persons—the triune God with his church.

What is the theological import of understanding justification to be a participation in the justified Christ? First, by locating justification itself in Christ, it establishes and upholds the *alien* character of both righteousness and justification itself. Second, this protects against the possibility of meriting justification by changing the nature of the question. For Edwards, the question is not, "How can I become righteous and therefore justified?" but is instead, "How can I become united to Christ, where righteousness and justification reside?" As already highlighted, the key question in this schema becomes the nature of the union and its relation to faith. As long as the union itself is not meritorious or virtuous in any way, or, more poignantly, is not *taken to be so*, then Edwards can protect against "Arminian" opponents. Third, Edwards's doctrine of justification is therefore "thin" (or "walled off" as Horton would have it), because the declaration of justification itself does not have transformative power. Fourth, given these three implications of his view, Edwards reconceives the nature of the declaration of justification. Instead of a gratuitously gracious declaration that constitutes a reality which is not (making righteous the unrighteous), God *qua* judge simply declares what is true: believers are righteous through the legal union they have with Christ. As we see below, Edwards does not undermine God's constituting speech act, or its gratuitously gracious nature, but simply moves its doctrinal location. Theologically, Christ is the center around which all soteriological loci find their orbit. The Spirit, as we turn to now, applies this work by uniting to Christ,

---

[48] "Treatise on Grace," *WJE*, 21:188.
[49] Ibid.

illuminating Christ to the elect, and infusing them with divine love, grace, and holiness.

The Doctrine of Regeneration

Edwards organizes the questions of redemption around his Trinitarian conception of "purchase," and delineates the issues of justification based upon a participation in Christ's own justification. Here, we consider how justification relates to regeneration in an attempt to highlight how Edwards's language of faith, union, and infusion interrelate in the overall picture he paints of God's redeeming work. If our brief development of Edwards's account of justification focused almost solely on christology, our account here will turn our attention to pneumatology. Edwards's doctrine of justification, as outlined in *Justification by Faith*, emphasizes the former over the latter. The doctrine of justification is *primarily* concerned with *Christ's* justification in the *historia salutis*, and only secondarily with the fact that Christ's justification is available to humanity through faith (delineated in the *ordo salutis*), as faith unites to Christ (by his Spirit). In other words, Edwards's doctrine of justification provides adequate grounding for the application of redemption and its accomplishment in Christ. This protects against, in the words of Richard Gaffin, focusing on the "ordo at the expense of the salutis."[50] The movement of redemption is God's twofold movement in Word and Spirit to redeem the elect: the life of Christ as the righteous one who is justified, and the uniting of believers by the Spirit to Christ by whom they participate in Christ's justification and receive the benefits of his redemption. Our attention here now falls upon the latter as we ask how Christ's accomplished redemption is applied to the elect.

Richard Muller provides a terse definition of the doctrine of regeneration: "the rebirth of mind and will accomplished by the gracious work of the Holy Spirit at the outset of the *ordo salutis*."[51]

---

[50] Richard B. Gaffin Jr., "Biblical Theology and the Westminster Standards," Beginning with Moses, http://beginningwithmoses.org/bt-articles/188/biblical-theology-and-the-westminster-standards.
[51] Richard A. Muller, "Regeneratio," in *Dictionary of Latin and Greek Theological Terms: Drawn Principally from Protestant Scholastic Theology* (Grand Rapids, MI: Baker Academic, 1985), 259.

Edwards himself offers similar declarations, linking regeneration with being "born again," "repentance," and "conversion." He states that, "by regeneration, or being begotten or born again, the same change in the state of the mind is signified, with that which the Scripture speaks of as effected in true repentance and conversion."[52] Furthermore, Edwards continues by adding, "[t]he change the mind passes under in repentance and conversion, is that in which saving *faith* is attained."[53] Maybe more provocatively, Edwards claims that in the act of regeneration "habits of true virtue and holiness" are obtained and "men come to have the character of true Christians."[54]

If, as Muller suggests, regeneration stands at the forefront of the *ordo salutis*, and in regeneration believers come to have habits of holiness and even the character of a Christian, it could seem as if God declares righteous those who are, in fact, righteous through regeneration and not union with Christ. Furthermore, Edwards states explicitly:

> For first, there must be an idea of Jesus Christ in the mind, that is an agreeable and truly lovely idea to him; but this cannot be before the soul is sanctified. There must also be the acts of true belief, of his willingness to receive, etc.; neither can this be before sanctification. There must also be a hatred of sin before Christ can be received as a Savior from sin; neither can this be without sanctification.[55]

In the application of redemption, Christ is no less central

---

[52] "Original Sin," *WJE*, 3:361–62.

[53] Ibid., 362 (emphasis in original).

[54] Ibid., 363.

[55] "The 'Miscellanies,' no. 77," *WJE*, 13:245. For parallel material in some of Edwards's favorite sources, see: Richard Sibbes, *Lydia's Conversion* in *The Works of Richard Sibbes*, vol. 6 (Edinburgh: Banner of Truth Trust, 1983), 525; John Owen, *The Holy Spirit*, 17 vols., *The Works of John Owen*, vol. 3 (London: Banner of Truth, 1966), 223. Van Mastricht seems to be utilizing the term "sanctification" in the same sense as Edwards when he states, "However, we mean not to deny here that it may be (and often is) the case that a sanctification of the Spirit, in a general sense comprehending vocation, regeneration, conversion, and sanctification properly so called, is effected at one and the same time." Peter van Mastricht, "A Treatise on Regeneration," in *Theologia Theoretica-Practica* (1699), anonymous English translation, ed. Brandon Withrow (Morgan, PA: Soli Deo Gloria, 2002), 27. For further discussion see, Schafer, "Jonathan Edwards and Justification by Faith," 59; Waddington, "Jonathan Edwards's 'Ambiguous and Somewhat Precarious' Doctrine of Justification," 365–67, esp. 365 fn29; Cherry, *The Theology of Jonathan Edwards*, 41–43; and McDermott, "Jonathan Edwards on Justification by Faith," 94–95.

than in its accomplishment, but now has authority over the Holy Spirit, based on his covenant with the Father in the *pactum salutis*, and sends his Spirit to apply his benefits.[56] Regeneration applies *broadly* to the purchase of the Holy Spirit, made by Christ, and given by him to the elect. In this purchase, there is one movement of the Spirit, which can be logically-delineated in three ways. First, the Spirit, as the love of God, is the bond of love which unites the elect to Christ.[57] It would even be fitting to say that Christ loves the elect to such a degree, even in the midst of their sin, that his love truly unites them to himself.[58] Second, and moving into regeneration more *narrowly* conceived, the Spirit illumines the person so that he can rationally respond to Christ as Savior and Lord. Third, the Spirit is infused into the person as grace itself. Note that on Edwards's account the Spirit is the love of God and grace itself, and therefore *is* the believer's "disposition" or "habit" of grace.[59]

As we have already shown, in Edwards's view fallen people cannot be justified except through a participation in Christ's own justification. Edwards's doctrine of justification stands and falls with his concept of union. Union, according to Edwards, is had by faith, and humanity, furthermore, are treated as rational creatures. For a believer to have faith there has to be a movement of the Spirit to illumine a person so that he/she can truly receive Christ, since faith entails apprehension (understanding)

[56] Jonathan Edwards, "The 'Miscellanies,' no. 1060," in *WJE*, vol. 20, *The "Miscellanies" 833–1152*, ed. Amy Plantinga Pauw (New Haven, CT: Yale University Press, 2002), 427.

[57] Van Mastricht states that, "Regeneration conveys that power into the soul by which the person who is to be saved is enabled to receive the offer." Van Mastricht, "A Treatise on Regeneration," 12. This broad sense is how we are taking the term here. Van Mastricht continues to outline the stricter sense, "In this sense it means the same as the circumcision of the heart, as taking away the heart of stone and putting within us a heart of flesh, as a new creation, as drawing, as illumination, as turning the will, and especially as a spiritual resurrection and quickening." Ibid.

[58] This is the major point of Edwards's last reflections on imputation and satisfaction. See "The 'Miscellanies,' nos. 1352 and 1360," *WJE*, 23:481–92; 713–16. Likewise, "The Spirit of God is a spirit of love. And therefore when the Spirit of God enters into the soul, love enters. God is love, and he who has God dwelling in him by his Spirit will have love dwelling in him. The nature of the Holy Spirit is love; and it is by communicating himself, or his own nature, that the hearts of the saints are filled with love or charity." "Charity and Its Fruits," *WJE*, 8:132.

[59] This is in contrast to Michael McClenahan, who rightfully notes that the "foundation laid in the soul" and the infusion of the Spirit are distinct, but who fails to follow Edwards's argument concerning the Spirit *qua* disposition. See McClenahan, "Jonathan Edwards' Doctrine of Justification," 294–96.

and will. In this way Edwards's development of illumination influences justification by *faith* alone: the illuminating presence of the Spirit is logically necessary for faith to arise. Being united to Christ by his Spirit necessitates creaturely response, a "closing" with Christ. This act, again, is not regarded by God as having moral "fitness," but "natural" (not accepted for its own value as such). As Edwards explains in his *Religious Affections*, "It is not the worthiness or amiableness of our works, or anything in us, which recommends us to an interest in Christ and his benefits."[60] If faith is considered as holy or moral for justification, Edwards is clear that the scheme would then be based on works rather than faith.[61] Therefore, for an ungodly, unrighteous, and depraved person to close with Christ, he needs an illumination of their minds.

> . . . one glimpse of the moral and spiritual glory of God, and supreme amiableness of Jesus Christ, shining into the heart, overcomes and abolishes this opposition, and inclines the soul to Christ, as it were, by an omnipotent power: so that now, not only the understanding, but the will, and the whole soul receives and embraces the Savior. This is most certainly the discovery, which is the first internal foundation of a saving faith in Christ. . . .
>
> The sense of divine beauty, is the first thing in the actual change made in the soul, in true conversion, and is the foundation of everything else belonging to that change; as is evident by those words of the Apostle, II Cor. 3:18, "But we all with open face, beholding as in a glass, the glory of the Lord, are changed

---

[60] Jonathan Edwards, "A Treatise Concerning Religious Affections," in *WJE*, vol. 2, *Religious Affections*, ed. John E. Smith (New Haven, CT: Yale University Press, 1959), 455. Just prior Edwards states, "And this is the notion of justification without works (as this doctrine is taught in the Scripture) that it is not the worthiness or loveliness of our works, or anything in us, which is in any wise accepted with God, as a balance for the guilt of sin, or a recommendation of sinners to his acceptance as heirs of life." Ibid. One of the main concerns for Edwards throughout the discourse is how believers have faith, which is a virtue, but is not rendered worthy in any way. In what is called the "Gazeteer Notebook," Edwards states, "It is [not] whether faith, or any other acts of works of ours, interests us as our good works . . . but whether it be only by virtue of the relation it bears to Christ as a proper receiving of him. He that is orthodox holds that our holy practice interests us only this way, viz. as it is an expression of our receiving Christ. The others hold that faith justifies only by virtue of its loveliness." Jonathan Edwards, *Documents on the Trinity, Grace and Faith*, "Book of Minutes on the Arminian Controversy" in *The Works of Jonathan Edwards Online*, vol. 37 (Jonathan Edwards Center, Yale University, 2008).
[61] "Religious Affections," *WJE*, 2:457.

into the same image, from glory to glory, even as by the Spirit of the Lord."[62]

Christ's first act in applying his redeeming work to individual members of his elect community is to unveil himself to them. This sight is only available to humanity through the Spirit's work of illumination; in a single moment of illumination the person is brought to saving faith in Christ, which "closes" the legal union, making faith the marital equivalent of saying "I do." Logically, therefore, illumination is prior to justification, since illumination is the necessary foundation for faith, and faith for union.[63] Furthermore, it is noteworthy that Edwards claims that "conversion is wrought at once," and while "reformation and conviction that is preparatory to conversion may be gradual . . . yet that work of grace upon the soul whereby a person is brought out of a state of total corruption and depravity into a state of grace . . . is in a moment."[64] Likewise, Edwards speaks of new birth, regeneration, calling, and "opening the eyes of the blind" as synonyms for conversion.[65] Therefore, in one moment, someone who is ungodly is converted, adopted, and justified. This point should not be underemphasized. Edwards's logical delineation does not change the fact that conversion, with all its facets, is a single moment.

There is then, on Edwards's view, a twofold declaration, only one of which constitutes transformation. God declares the sinner regenerated, in a truly constitutive declaration, and only

---

[62] Jonathan Edwards, "True Grace," in *WJE*, vol. 25, *Sermons and Discourses 1743–1758*, ed. Wilson H. Kimnach (New Haven, CT: Yale University Press, 2006), 635–36. Also: "Indeed the first act of the Spirit of God, or the first that this divine temper exerts itself in, is in spiritual understanding, or in the sense of the mind, its perception of glory and excellency, etc. in the ideas it has of divine things; and this is before any proper acts of the will. Indeed, the inclination of the soul is as immediately exercised in that sense of the mind which is called spiritual understanding, as the intellect. For it is not only the mere presence of ideas in the mind, but it is the mind's sense of their excellency, glory and delightfulness." "The 'Miscellanies,' no. 397," *WJE*, 13:463.

[63] "This light is such as effectually influences the inclination, and changes the nature of the soul. It assimilates the nature to the divine nature, and changes the soul into an image of the same glory that is beheld. . . . This light, and this only, will bring the soul to a saving close with Christ." Jonathan Edwards, "A Divine and Supernatural Light," in *WJE*, vol. 17, *Ethical Writings*, ed. Mark Valeri (New Haven, CT: Yale University Press, 1999), 424.

[64] "A Treatise on Grace," *WJE*, 21:161.

[65] Ibid., 160–61.

then declares the sinner righteous (a declaration dependent upon the "real" union). Edwards claims, "[I]n creation, something is brought out of nothing in an instant. God speaks and it is done," while in regeneration, Christ, "through his great power, does *but speak the powerful word and it is done*, he does but call and the heart of the sinner immediately comes."[66] It is not the declaration of justification which constitutes creaturely righteousness, but instead, the parallel to God's speaking creation into being is his declaration of *new* creation—regeneration. God's efficacious call is the constitutive speech act that brings about faith, thereby grounding justification itself.[67] God's call to the sinner is sending his Spirit to instantaneously unite, illuminate, and infuse himself as a principle for future holiness and action within the person, thus opening his eyes to grasp onto Christ, where redemption truly lies. This work in regeneration does not somehow give a person leverage for salvation. Rather, regeneration is that part of God's call that allows a sinner to see and grasp Christ by faith alone.

As noted, believers only have an interest in Christ by *seeing* Christ and embracing him, which is the very act of faith and union. While it is possible to make logical and semantic delineations between regeneration, conversion, justification, and adoption, they are in fact wrought through one act of Christ upon the soul of the unregenerate through a giving of his Spirit. This Spirit, as love and grace itself, unites to Christ, illumines Christ, and works the very love of Christ (that is, love to Christ and Christ's own love) into the heart of this person:

> So that true saving grace is no other than that very love of God; that is, God, in one of the persons of the Trinity, uniting himself to the soul of a creature as a vital principle, dwelling there and

---

[66] Ibid., 161–62 (emphasis added).
[67] In "The 'Miscellanies,' no. 417" on "free grace," Edwards provides three ways a gift may be freely bestowed: (1) with no prerequisite qualification or condition; (2) with a "suitableness in the nature and inclination of the subject," which allows for harmony with the gift bestowed; and (3) if the gift is given for the "actual exercise" of "agreeableness" and "suitableness of nature and inclination" in accepting and "closing" with the offer. Edwards then suggests that the efficacious call follows the first, while justification and salvation follow the latter two, because faith is necessary. WJE, 13:476.

exerting himself by the faculties of the soul of man, in his own proper nature, after the manner of a principle of nature.[68]

This shifts attention from the Spirit *qua* illuminator to the Spirit *qua* "principle of grace." The Spirit, though one, has diverse actions, and therefore it is important to demarcate between the Spirit's work of infusion, leading to holiness, with union, leading to justification.[69] Muller states: "The Protestant scholastics deny that *gratia infusa* or *gratia inhaerens*, inhering grace, is the basis of justification. Rather *gratia infusa* is the result of *regeneratio* and the basis of sanctification, the source of all the good works of believers."[70] Muller's point highlights Edwards's concerns perfectly.[71] For Edwards, the Spirit's presence is the primary vehicle for redemption, while the secondary focus is union, illumination, and infusion—union leading to justification, illumination to faith, and infusion to sanctification (sanctification depending on the other two).[72] Edwards stresses the *one* action of conver-

---

[68] "A Treatise on Grace," *WJE*, 21:194.

[69] Anri Morimoto pounces on these concepts in Edwards's thought, arguing that salvation depends upon an infusion of grace, rather than, as outlined above, union with Christ. The Reformed delineation of the terms "calling," "regeneration," "conversion," and "sanctification," Morimoto suggests, for Edwards, "all mean the same reality of grace infused at one stance." Anri Morimoto, *Jonathan Edwards and the Catholic Vision of Salvation* (University Park, PA: The Pennsylvania University Press, 1995), 31. Morimoto shows his confusion by placing all of these concepts in infusion rather than in pneumatology broadly considered. His move to do so is reductionistic, and fails to delineate the Spirit's work of illumination as logically distinct from infusion. Admittedly, the mistake to focus on one infusion, rather than one work of the Spirit, is not without warrant. Edwards states, "There is not one conversion to bring the heart to faith, and another to infuse love to God, and another humility, and another repentance, and another love to men. But all are given in one work of the Spirit. All these things are infused by one conversion, one change of the heart; which argues that all the graces are united and linked together, as being contained in that one and the same new nature which is given in regeneration." "Charity and Its Fruits," *WJE*, 8:332. There is truly a new nature given in regeneration, and that is *the Spirit*. The emphasis is on the Spirit as the one who works, and not to reduce infusion to be the sole working of the Spirit.

[70] Muller, "Gratia Infusa," in *Dictionary of Latin and Greek Theological Terms*, 131. Waddington makes a similar point; see Waddington, "Jonathan Edwards's 'Ambiguous and Somewhat Precarious' Doctrine of Justification," 359–60 fn8.

[71] Michael Horton states, "Even if it is granted that justification is an exclusively forensic declaration, the rest of the *ordo* has sometimes been treated even in Reformed theology as the consequence of an entirely different event—namely, an infusion of a new *habitus* (disposition) prior to effectual calling." Horton, *Covenant and Salvation*, 216. Edwards would not fall into this exact caricature. Edwards focuses, not on infusion as such, but on the Spirit whose nature and work apply Christ's work. It is still the *Word* of God entering the heart, but it is by the Spirit of God that it does enter and is efficacious.

[72] This is, admittedly, an oversimplification; my main point of emphasis is on infusion and illumination as logically distinct from union, just as conversion and sanctification are logically distinct from justification.

sion—but while there is a single moment of conversion, there is also a gradual work of grace postconversion in sanctification.[73] To avoid bifurcating justification and sanctification, Edwards understands them as two distinct benefits received through Christ's sending of the Spirit. The focus, again, is on the Spirit *given* rather than the benefits *received*. Union, for example, serves to delineate how the elect, by the *Spirit*, are united to *Christ*. Admittedly, on Edwards's view, there is only a subtle distinction between the Spirit and the Spirit's benefits, since the work of the Spirit entails the Spirit communicating his "nature" (i.e., holiness, beauty, grace, etc.).

In purchasing the Spirit, Christ does much more than purchase justification for his people. He purchases redemption and reconciliation to God in Christ. Christ continues to be the centerpiece of redemption, so that he "became to us wisdom from God, righteousness and sanctification and redemption" (1 Cor. 1:30). It is by Christ alone that believers have righteousness, and "'tis by being in him that we are justified, have our sins pardoned, and are received as righteous into God's favor." Christ is, furthermore, "made unto us inherent as well as imputed righteousness."[74] Redemption, for Edwards, is developed primarily through an emphasis on the movement of Word and Spirit in the economy, with a second order discussion parsing the reality of that economic movement. Edwards explains the primary and secondary (or "second order") discussions this way: "Christ the Mediator, by whom, and his righteousness, by which we are justified, *is more directly* the object of this acceptance, and justification which is the benefit arising therefrom, more indirectly."[75] The answer to

---

[73] "The graces of Christianity are all from the Spirit of God sent forth into the heart, and dwelling there as an holy principle and divine nature. And therefore all graces are only the different ways of acting of the same divine nature, as there may be different reflections of the light of the sun. But it is all the same kind of light originally, because it all comes from the same fountain, the same body of light." "Charity and Its Fruits," *WJE*, 8:332. Likewise, "This doctrine, and what has been said under it, may in some measure show us how this is; for by this we learn that all the graces of Christianity are infused in this, inasmuch as all are concatenated; when one is infused, all are infused; there is not one grace wanting. A [convert] at the same moment that he is become such is possessed of all holy principles, all gracious dispositions." Ibid., 334.

[74] "God Glorified in Man's Dependence," *WJE*, 17:201.

[75] "Justification by Faith Alone," *WJE*, 19:153 (emphasis added).

the question *How are believers saved?* is always Christ and Christ's purchase of his Spirit:

> What is it that is the beginning or earnest of eternal life in the soul, but spiritual life? And what is that but grace? The inheritance that Christ has purchased for the elect, *is the Spirit of God* . . . in his vital indwelling in the heart, exerting and communicating himself there, in his own proper, holy or divine nature: and this is *the sum total* of the inheritance that Christ purchased for the elect.[76]

The sum total of a believer's inheritance is the Spirit, who is given to unite them to Christ (justification) and to illumine and infuse (regeneration). As a movement of Word and Spirit, redemption is parsed through union, illumination, and infusion, which delineate *how Christ redeems by his Spirit.*[77] In uniting believers to himself by his Spirit, God declares them legally one with Christ and able to receive his righteousness as if it were their own. By illuminating the hearts of fallen people through his Spirit, Christ himself is illumined to them, and believers freely and rationally grasp onto him as their Savior with union through faith. In the same act, furthermore, Christ gives grace, not only to unite and illuminate, but to continue to follow—what Edwards calls evan-

---

[76] "Religious Affections," *WJE*, 2:236 (emphasis added). These "second order" discussions can be seen in the following passage where Edwards offers his typical emphasis on Christ and the Spirit rather than on specific loci in the *ordo*: "The soul [of a saint] is joined to Christ and they are made one. As the water enters into the roots [of the tree], so Christ enters the heart and soul of a godly man and dwells there. The Spirit of Christ comes into the very heart of a saint as water to the roots of a tree. . . . Water gives life and keeps it alive; so [Christ enlivens the heart and] makes it grow: makes it grow beautiful [and] fruitful." "Christ Is to the Heart Like a River to a Tree Planted by It," *WJE*, 25:603.

[77] Morimoto, in my opinion, neglects Edwards's own emphasis, when he claims, "As far as one can see from this, the basic structure of Edwards's soteriology is an ontological transition from the state of corruption to the state of salvation—much like in Roman Catholic soteriology." Morimoto, *Jonathan Edwards and the Catholic Vision of Salvation*, 73. Furthermore, on such grounds, Morimoto questions if Edwards's theology really has a place for a doctrine of justification, and rhetorically asks, "What significance can legal imputation bear in a system that holds the ontological transformation of the human state in such high regard?" Ibid., 74. As we have seen above, this question fails to understand the nature of the justification question. Justification seeks to explain how the unrighteous are both free from guilt and declared righteous, which, for Edwards, necessitates more than a "legal fiction," and outlines how believers have righteousness that can truly be seen as their own. Furthermore, Morimoto confuses the issues when he pushes the pneumatological into the realm of the ontological and reduces justification to soteriology broadly considered. No Reformed account of justification limits the Spirit's actual work in the soul in regeneration, and Edwards is no closer to Roman Catholic soteriology for following suit.

gelical obedience—a life lived with the Spirit infused as grace itself, functioning as a principle or disposition of holiness in the believer.[78] United to Christ and having Christ's own love infused into their souls (i.e., the Holy Spirit), the regenerate participate in God's own excellence.[79]

Conclusion

Far from ignoring or undermining the forensic nature of justification, Edwards is concerned to delineate redemption by Word and Spirit, which necessarily entails a forensic justification. Edwards's theologizing quickly moves away from justification because justification is primarily a hinge point in the doctrines of redemption, securing the status of the elect as righteous, forgiven, and redeemed. Edwards's emphasis on the subsequent outworking of that redemption does not, in any way, undermine the importance of justification. Many confuse Edwards's emphasis because they fail to locate the discussion appropriately. Edwards's most "theologically weighty" claim concerns the fact that salvation is found only in Christ and is available only by the Spirit. That reality governs his entire soteriology. The "material weight" of Edwards's discussion (what Edwards talks most about) may very well be the Spirit's work in the soul, but locating redemption in this latter material fails to grasp the nature of his argument and primary dogmatic claims. Salvation exists only in Christ, and therefore the doctrines of salvation are all oriented by Christ's person and work, and then, secondarily, are oriented by how the Spirit applies those benefits to the elect.

Edwards locates justification in a broader movement of the Son to obtain justification, sanctification, and ultimately glorifi-

---

[78] "By his producing this effect the Spirit becomes an indwelling vital principle in the soul, and the subject becomes a spiritual being, denominated so from the Spirit of God which dwells in him and of whose nature he is a partaker [II Pet. 1:4]." "Charity and Its Fruits," *WJE*, 8:158.

[79] "They have spiritual excellency and joy by a kind of participation of God. They are made excellent by a communication of God's excellency: God put his own beauty, i.e. his beautiful likeness, upon their souls. . . . The saints hath spiritual joy and pleasure by a kind of effusion of God on the soul. . . . The saints have both their spiritual excellency and blessedness by the gift of the Holy Ghost, or Spirit of God, and his dwelling in them. They are not only caused by the Holy Ghost, but are in the Holy Ghost as their principle. The Holy Spirit becoming an inhabitant is a vital principle in the soul." "God Glorified in Man's Dependence," *WJE*, 17:208 (emphasis added).

cation in his own person. Edwards continually pushes questions concerning redemption back to Christ's person and work, using participation and regeneration as ways to bypass attacks against the Reformed position as promoting "legal fictions." In doing so, Edwards attempts to keep hold of a constituting declaration (located in the efficacious call), faith preceding justification and an unwavering bond between justification and sanctification by focusing the *ordo salutis* on Christ's gracious giving over the purchase made—the Holy Spirit of God. Bruce McCormack, speaking of the move to locate regeneration logically prior to justification, states, "For where regeneration is made—even if only logically—to be the root of justification, there the work of God 'in us' is, once again (and now on the soil of the Reformation!) made to be the ground of the divine forgiveness of sins."[80] Rather, for Edwards, the only true ground for forgiveness is Christ himself. Because salvation, in its entirety, is found in Christ, union, we could say, grounds the application of redemption. The work of God "in us" is for the reception of that gift through union. Edwards is concerned to uphold human faculties in salvation, such that they can receive Christ's free gift, but this move does not somehow relocate forgiveness to the human side of the equation. In the end, Edwards may not convince his critics, but he sets up a variety of safety measures in an attempt to protect his account against his opponents (e.g., justification through participation in Christ's justification, the moral/natural distinction, and an emphasis on the economy). Critiques of Edwards's position must take these emphases seriously, placing him firmly within a period of Reformed dogmatic work that delineated justification in broadly similar terms.

---

[80] Bruce McCormack, "What's At Stake in Current Debates Over Justification? The Crisis of Protestantism in the West," in *Justification: What's At Stake in the Current Debates*, ed. Mark Husbands and Daniel Treier (Downers Grove, IL: InterVarsity Press, 2004), 102.

CHAPTER THREE

The Gospel of Justification and Edwards's Social Vision

Rhys Bezzant

Significant moments in Jonathan Edwards's ministry were connected to his exposition of the doctrine of justification by faith. In concluding his studies at Yale College in 1723 in the midst of the contentions surrounding the theological defection of Rector Clap to the Anglicans, Edwards defended his AM with a disquisition on justification by grace through faith. As well, the beginnings of the surprising work of God in Northampton in 1734–1735 were, in Edwards's estimation, provoked by sermons from Romans 4:5: his own later descriptions in the *Faithful Narrative* of that localized revival give prominence to the doctrine of justification as a causal factor.[1] In Edwards's only publication of sermons during his lifetime, under the title of *Discourse on Various Important Subjects* (1738), the theme of justification, along with adapted sermons on justification from the Northampton revival, forms the *leitmotif*.[2] An early nineteenth-century chronicler comments: "There was, then, in 1734 at Northampton and generally in New England, a special need of such sermons as Edwards preached;

---

[1] Jonathan Edwards, "A Faithful Narrative," in *The Works of Jonathan Edwards* (hereafter WJE),vol. 4, *The Great Awakening*, ed. C. C. Goen (New Haven, CT: Yale University Press, 1972), 148–49. In placing Edwards within the section on Puritan debates on justification, it is remarkable that McGrath attributes the impact of these sermons not to their content, for "they contained nothing which could be described as radical innovations," but rather it was "the earnestness with which they were preached" which led to "their astonishing and celebrated effects." Alister E. McGrath, *Iustitia Dei: A History of the Christian Doctrine of Justification* (Cambridge, UK: Cambridge University Press, 2005), 290.

[2] See Jonathan Edwards, "Preface to *Discourses on Various Important Subjects*," in WJE, vol. 19, *Sermons and Discourses 1734–1738*, ed. M. X. Lesser (New Haven, CT and London: Yale University Press, 2001), 793–98. This preface, written by Edwards, provides phrases that I have used in this chapter as apt headings to summarize Edwards's approach to doctrinal and historical concerns.

a special fitness in those sermons, to produce the effects which followed them."[3]

Edwards's own notebooks were also full of references to grace, faith, and justification, and one of the last miscellaneous essays, no. 1354, was devoted to this topic in 1756/1757.[4] His "Controversies" notebook, designed to provide resources for prosecuting his case against deism, contains a significant collection of essays on justification composed in the final phase of his career, from the late 1740s to the late 1750s.[5] It is not that justification was written about or preached by Edwards more frequently than any other theological locus; nevertheless this doctrine remains a theological signpost to the controversies and context of his ministry career in as far as his ruminations emerge at critical junctures.[6]

It is therefore the contention of this essay that Edwards's teaching on justification provides us not only with insights into his theological pedigree and systematic convictions, but also gives us a window into his ministry context and social location. In Puritan New England, espousing certain theological confessions was intricately connected to communal values and norms, and conversely doctrinal aberrations were easily identified with social declension or betrayal. The revivals themselves, which Edwards connects to the preaching of justification, were therefore understood not merely as the awakening of slumbering individuals, but ultimately as the reformation of families and communities, perhaps even of the nation. Indeed, the conceptualities of the covenant undergird much of Edwards's theological project, which form a loyal alliance with the doctrine of justification.

These very themes are drawn together by the apostle Paul

---

[3] Joseph Tracy, *The Great Awakening: A History of the Revival of Religion in the Time of Edwards and Whitefield* (Edinburgh: Banner of Truth Trust, 1976), 11–12.

[4] Jonathan Edwards, "The 'Miscellanies,' no. 1354," in *WJE*, vol. 23, *The "Miscellanies," 1153–1360*, ed. D. A. Sweeney (New Haven, CT and London: Yale University Press, 2004), 506–43.

[5] Jonathan Edwards, "'Controversies' Notebook: Justification," in *WJE*, vol. 21, *Writings on the Trinity, Grace and Faith*, ed. S. H. Lee (New Haven, CT and London: Yale University Press, 2003), 328–413.

[6] Justification is a lifelong preoccupation for Edwards because the refutation of Arminianism was a lifelong concern. See Avihu Zakai, *Jonathan Edwards's Philosophy of History: The Reenchantment of the World in the Age of Enlightenment* (Princeton: University Press, 2003), 35.

when he asserts that being made competent for a *ministry of justification* is equivalent to being prepared for a *ministry of the new covenant*, a ministry that gives life, drawing from the Spirit, and culminating in glory for "all of us" (2 Corinthians 3). It is negligent to atomize the impact of Edwards's doctrinal preaching, permitting only doctrinal outcomes. It is conversely fruitful to understand Edwards's soteriological vision issuing in the transformation of the social world. The gospel that Edwards preached was designed both to revive and to reform.

"A New Way of Acceptance": Justification Explained to Christians

The contours of Edwards's systematic reflection on justification are formative for his consequent revivalist agenda and social vision. While particular debates concerning justification will be rehearsed elsewhere in this volume, it remains to sketch them here for the sake of the argument that follows. Edwards explains justification by grace through faith within a larger theological context.

It must first be noted that Edwards sets justification within the broader sweep of the life, death, and resurrection of Christ, not with reference to the atonement alone. Though Christ offered himself supremely to the will of God on that great day of the Lord, when he submitted to his Father's particular will to drink the cup of wrath set before him, it is also true to say that the righteous requirements of the law were achieved in each day of Christ's incarnate life, as he offered faithful obedience to his Father. Christ's passive righteousness in his death and active righteousness in his life together qualify him as a fitting sacrifice for sins. Consider Edwards's Masters defense based his understanding of imputed righteousness on such christological commitments:

> There can be no doubt that justification is a certain act of positive favor that not only frees a person from sin but is also understood in fact as the approval of him as righteous through the righteous-

ness of Christ, both active and passive in both obedience and satisfaction.[7]

Edwards later asseverates in a sermon:

There are those that deny that Christ's active obedience to God's law is imputed to believers, or that it is any way available to their justification any otherwise than as a necessary qualification in order to render his sacrifice available. But 'tis very evident that Christ's active righteousness was necessary in order to our justification as well as his passive [righteousness].[8]

Significantly, Edwards creates a turning point in the *History of the Work of Redemption* not out of Christ's death alone, but out of the whole period of Christ's incarnate life, from his conception to his ascension, through which he fulfilled all righteousness.[9] The comprehensive character of Edwards's formulation of justification is likewise to be seen when he joins together the Christian believer's *freedom from* God's wrath with *reception of* "divine favor."[10] Justification speaks both to our enslaved past and our glorious future:

A person is said to be justified when he is approved of God as free from the guilt of sin, and its deserved punishment, and as having that *righteousness belonging to him that entitles to the reward of life.* . . . Some suppose that nothing more is intended in Scripture by justification than barely the remission of sins. . . . But that a believer's justification implies not only remission of sins, or acquittance from the wrath due to it, but also an admittance

---

[7] Jonathan Edwards, "A Sinner Is Not Justified in the Sight of God Except through the Righteousness of Christ Obtained by Faith," in *WJE*, vol. 14, *Sermons and Discourses 1723–1729*, ed. K. P. Minkema (New Haven, CT: Yale University Press, 1997), 60.

[8] "The Threefold Work of the Holy Spirit," *WJE*, 14:396–97.

[9] Jonathan Edwards, *WJE*, vol. 9, *A History of the Work of Redemption* (New Haven, CT: Yale University Press, 1989), 295. Sermons 14–17 in this series form a unit, representing the second and central phase of the work of redemption, which is the ministry of Christ in his humiliation before his exaltation. The common Puritan concern to understand *redemption* in terms of the pastoral application of justification is here revised, for *redemption*, though appropriated by individuals in justification, concerns the larger design of God from the fall to the consummation. See W. Reginald Ward, *Early Evangelicalism: A Global Intellectual History, 1670–1789* (Cambridge: University Press, 2006), 149–50.

[10] "Sinner Is Not Justified," *WJE*, 14:60. See also Stephen R. Holmes, *God of Grace and God of Glory: An Account of the Theology of Jonathan Edwards* (Edinburgh: T&T Clark, 2000), 142ff.

to a title to that glory that is the *reward of righteousness*, is more directly taught in the Scripture.[11]

There are in these strong statements forward-looking outworkings of our justified status, and the expectation of righteous living now that connects to our future reward (even if concrete social ramifications are here still muted). A positive model of the righteous life is subsumed within his conception of justification.[12] Conrad Cherry summarizes Edwards's thought in these ways:

> For our purposes what is significant in his [Edwards's] theory of the "at-one-ment" accomplished between God and man is the way in which the notion of imputation of righteousness is developed according to Christ's two major functions in relation to divine justice. Christ by his righteousness both satisfies the punitive demands of the law for sin and positively fulfils the law in order to achieve the atonement. The former he accomplishes through his sufferings, the latter through his perfect obedience unto death.[13]

It is in a more global defense of justification by faith that Edwards makes a clear connection with transformed living. For example, he sees no contrariety between the message of Paul and of James, for we may be justified through a gracious act of God, without our deserving or our contribution, which is not to preclude the active exercise of our faith.[14] Edwards makes the distinction between faith rightly viewed as a *condition* of our justification, even when it will never be the *cause* of our justification. In just the same way, our own obedience, a life of good works for which we were chosen, necessarily accompanies our justification as its condition, without invoking accusations of works-righteousness.

---

[11] "Justification by Faith Alone," *WJE*, 19:150–51 (emphasis added).

[12] Logan draws attention to the immorality that was endemic to the frontier and its lawlessness. Such background sharpens comments by Edwards concerning moral transformation and the place of his sermons on justification in the outworking of revival. See Samuel T. Logan Jr., "Jonathan Edwards and the 1734–35 Northampton Revival," in *The Practical Calvinist: An Introduction to the Presbyterian and Reformed Heritage*, ed. P. A. Lillback (Fearn, UK: Christian Focus, 2002), 240, 248.

[13] Conrad Cherry, *The Theology of Jonathan Edwards: A Reappraisal* (Bloomington, IN: Indiana University Press, 1990), 93.

[14] Edwards quotes from Rawlin, Turretin, Grotius, and Beza to support his case. See "'Controversies' Notebook," *WJE*, 21:343–44.

Much of the attention of Edwards in his writings on justification is occupied by this very debate generated by Arminianism and resolved through a nuanced appraisal of Enlightenment debates concerning causation.[15] It is in the end our union with Christ, which for Edwards (as for Calvin[16]) generates the proper foundation of both our justification and our sanctification:

> God don't give those that believe, an union *with*, or an interest *in* the Savior, in reward for faith, but only because faith is the soul's active uniting with Christ, or is itself the very act of unition, on their part . . . what is real in the union between Christ and his people, is the foundation of what is legal; that is, it is something really in them, and between them, uniting them, that is the ground of the suitableness of their being accounted as one by the Judge.[17]

Furthermore, with reference to union with Christ and our justified status, Edwards repeatedly appeals to the language of something being *fitting* or *suitable*, taking its rightful place within the divine ordering of the world, which does not necessarily admit of cause and effect, or antecedence and subsequence.[18] Faith fulfills just such a role as naturally *fitted* to union and justification, without actually *causing* them. There is a larger eschatological purpose of God and settled theological character of God which suggest the appropriate stability of this arrangement:

> God will neither look on Christ's merits as ours, nor adjudge his benefits to us, till we be *in* Christ: nor will he look upon us as being *in* him, without an active unition of our hearts and souls to him; because he is a wise being, and delights in order, and not in confusion, and that things should be together or asunder

---

[15] Sang Hyun Lee, "Grace and Justification by Faith Alone," in *The Princeton Companion to Jonathan Edwards*, ed. S. H. Lee (Princeton and Oxford: Princeton University Press, 2005), 145.

[16] Samuel T. Logan Jr., "The Doctrine of Justification in the Theology of Jonathan Edwards," *Westminster Theological Journal* 46/1 (1984): 26–52, esp. 35.

[17] "Justification by Faith Alone," *WJE*, 19:158. Logan expands on this distinction between cause and condition, and places it within a larger historical framework. See Logan, "The Doctrine of Justification," esp. 30–35.

[18] Alan Heimert, *Religion and the American Mind: From the Great Awakening to the Revolution*, The Jonathan Edwards Classic Studies Series (Eugene, OR: Wipf & Stock, 2006), 73. For Edwards, a sequence is not essentially a cause with a necessary effect.

according to their nature; and his making such a constitution is a testimony of his love of order.[19]

While maintaining God's ultimate freedom to give salvation as a gift, Edwards introduces an intellectualist framework for soteriology, in which assumptions concerning the predictable appropriation of salvation are admissible. The individual's salvation is not essentially a disorderly intrusion upon reality, but is rather connected to Edwards's "overall theological vision" and the (re-) ordering of all reality which is God's ultimate purpose, design, and delight.[20] To be an advocate of justification is therefore to appeal, even if only implicitly, to a larger concern for a corporate reality that is bigger than the individual's own redemption. Justification flags not just revival but renovation of the world.[21]

Such a view of justification is therefore consolidated by Edwards when he connects it to *covenant theology*. Perry Miller made popular in the middle of the twentieth century the view that Edwards was *reneging* on the covenant or federal theology of his forebears, to take up the attractive and contemporary philosophy of Newton and Locke. Such a betrayal was evident, according to Miller, in "the scandal of Edwards' discourses on justification."[22] More recently, Miller's views have been revised, and greater acknowledgment of Edwards's commitment to the doctrine of the covenant has been expressed. Harry Stout draws our attention, for example, to the sermons preached by Edwards on days other than Sunday, such as on the occasion of military victories or national fasting, to highlight *covenant sensibilities*:

> Jonathan Edwards is often cited for his rejection of the old covenant theology. But that was in matters of sacraments, not national identity. While rejecting the Half-way Covenant and "mere" external morality as means of grace, Edwards never questioned

---

[19] "Justification by Faith Alone," *WJE*, 19:161.
[20] Lee, "Grace and Justification," 145.
[21] Indeed, justification of an individual proleptically announces the verdict of the judgment, and thereby foreshadows the resolution of all history (Rom. 2:13; 4:25; 5:9), when God will formally pass sentence and redeem creation (Rom. 8:21).
[22] Perry Miller, *Jonathan Edwards* (Lincoln, NE: University of Nebraska Press, 2005), 115.

New England's corporate identity as a special people bound in an external national covenant. . . . When facing outward enemies Edwards, like his peers, instinctively fell back on federal promises in their simplest, most elemental form.[23]

In fact, we have to look no further than the very discourses on justification to find Edwards making links between salvation and covenantal life. Carl Bogue avers that Edwards "sees the covenant of grace and justification by faith alone as descriptions of the same phenomena."[24] In describing the significance of justification to Christian theology, Edwards situates justification at the heart of the covenant of grace:

> The great and most distinguishing difference between that covenant [with Adam], and the covenant of grace is, that by the covenant of grace we are not thus justified by our own works, but only by faith in Jesus Christ. . . . And therefore the Apostle when he in the same epistle to the Galatians, speaks of the doctrine of justification by works as another gospel, he adds "which is not another" (1:6–7). 'Tis no gospel at all; 'tis law: 'tis no covenant of grace, but of works: 'tis not an evangelical, but a legal doctrine.[25]

Justification is received *through faith* as condition and not cause, so also justification is received *by grace*, as a gift and not of merit. However, while the covenant in which this gift is embedded can be delivered in different forms, Edwards is at pains to make clear that the substance of covenant conditions for justification are equivalent under old or new dispensations. Both the indicative and imperative of salvation flow out of the consistent covenantal character of God:

---

[23] Harry S. Stout, *The New England Soul: Preaching and Religious Culture in Colonial New England* (New York: Oxford University Press, 1986), 235–36. For example, a remarkable sermon preached on a fast day in 1738 upon the waning of the fervor of the revival makes plain Edwards's ownership of the national covenant. He says, "We are a covenant people . . . we are so in a special manner . . . And here God has entered into covenant with us." See Jonathan Edwards, "Indicting God," *WJE*, 19:759. According to Noll, Edwards holds loosely to the inherited notions of covenant as a totalizing narrative, without ever abandoning entirely their more limited usefulness. See Mark A. Noll, *America's God: From Jonathan Edwards to Abraham Lincoln* (Oxford: University Press, 2002), 44–50.
[24] Carl W. Bogue, *Jonathan Edwards and the Covenant of Grace* (Cherry Hill, NJ: Mack, 1975), 238.
[25] "Justification by Faith Alone," *WJE*, 19:239.

They are the same commands delivered in different manner: as the terms of the legal covenant, they were delivered with thunder and lightning; as the terms of the new covenant, 'tis with the sweet voice of the love of God.

That God hath so ordered the covenant of grace that it should agree with a mere covenant of works [in] that respect, that . . . justification is always connected with holiness in the person justified . . . arises from the holiness of God and from his love to holiness and hatred of sin. . . . Because God was holy, and delighted in holiness and hated sin, therefore he would appoint no way of justification but such as tended to promote holiness.[26]

The language of covenant serves to create a framework connecting holy demands with justified status, just as it gives objective ballast to the experience of faith and grace: it situates the experience of salvation within a biblical-historical framework, as well as within the particular narrative of Edwards's nation's life. As we shall see more explicitly in the following section, the doctrine of justification is for Edwards of singular importance not only for individual salvation, but also for the New England project in terms of its theological priority and its social ramifications. While some may presume that it must have been the preaching of hellfire that instigated the Connecticut River revivals of 1734–1735, there is little doubt in Edwards's mind that it was these sermons on justification, these "broadsides of pure and uncompromised Reformed doctrine,"[27] in the words of Clarence Goen, which proved to be the spark that lit the kindling, and the lens through which the revivals more broadly were to be understood.

"That Remarkable Season:" Justification Vindicated toward Opponents

In "that remarkable season" of 1734–1735, the whole town of Northampton was profoundly impacted by Edwards's preaching concerning justification. According to his later "Preface to the *Discourse on Various Important Subjects*," his preaching of justifica-

---

[26] "'Controversies' Notebook: Justification," *WJE*, 21:365.
[27] Clarence C. Goen, *Revivalism and Separatism in New England, 1740–1800: Strict Congregationalists and Separate Baptists in the Great Awakening* (Middletown, CT: Wesleyan University Press, 1987), 7.

tion served to promote both the conversion of individuals *and* the defense of the unique status of the New England project, for justification funded resistance, in differing measures, to the twin threats to the purity of Reformed doctrine and practice in the New World of the eighteenth century, namely Arminianism and antinomianism. Morimoto is at least right to argue that, for Edwards, justification is being used in these years as an anti-Arminian strategy.[28] However, it would be incorrect to see justification as *merely* a rhetorical device used by Edwards in later *post ipso facto* explanations of his successes, without acknowledging the ways in which his precise doctrinal formulation of justification achieved positive pastoral and social outcomes during the Connecticut River revival itself, which this section treats.

In preaching against that collection of beliefs known as "Arminianism," which defined the spirit of the age in the early eighteenth century,[29] Edwards took up intellectual arms against an amorphous group that had highlighted not only the positive role humans can perform in achieving salvation, but also the liberal notion that individuals are the indivisible unit of society.[30] As Robert Jenson asserts, Arminianism was "Protestantism without the Reformation,"[31] or the spirit of protest with neither doctrinal anchors nor social moorings. To combat Arminianism was to resist a social trend that would, if left to its own devices, undermine the corporate understanding of reality as received in New England.

Contemporaneously, both Arminians and the Reformed were anxious of the influence of *antinomianism*, which stressed the pos-

---

[28] A. Morimoto, *Jonathan Edwards and the Catholic Vision of Salvation* (University Park, PA: Pennsylvania State University Press, 1995), 71–101.

[29] Minkema summarizes the Arminian challenge in New England thus: "Arminianism was named after the sixteenth-century Dutch theologian Jacob Arminius. Originally, it was narrowly understood as a repudiation of John Calvin's supralapsarianism, but by the early eighteenth century the term came to encompass a broad spectrum of theologians, including the majority of the Anglican clergy, who emphasized good works over right doctrine and maintained the free will of humankind to accept or reject the grace of God." See Kenneth P. Minkema, "Preface to the Period," *WJE*, 14:17. It ought to be added that Roman Catholic encouragement of works-righteousness had been consistently resisted in Puritan preaching before the eighteenth century, which Edwards continued to address.

[30] Henry F. May, *The Enlightenment in America* (New York: Oxford University Press, 1976), 14.

[31] Robert W. Jenson, *America's Theologian: A Recommendation of Jonathan Edwards* (New York/Oxford: Oxford University Press, 1988), 54–55.

sibility of immediate assurance of salvation without reference to the shape of ethical living, or the separation of justification from sanctification. Such antinomianism was a threat to the received order, for some viewed it as antithetical to the need for growth in obedience and submission to social norms. It functioned as a visceral reminder of the disorder in the period of early New England settlement of the 1630s when Anne Hutchinson forsook the established authorities of Bible and tradition and pursued instead immediate spiritual discernment as her governing authority. Order was sacrificed on the altar of enthusiasm, or separatism was espoused in place of covenant and sacraments:

> Every pious New Englander cherished the experience of conversion, which certified the indwelling of the Spirit, but most also believed that spiritual immediacy could transform men into pneumatic enthusiasts. They knew also that ecclesiastical continuity required sacramental structures: infant baptism both symbolized and guaranteed the continuity of the Church covenant.[32]

If those dubbed "Arminian" or "Latitudinarian" were prone to collapse the transcendent into the immanent without remainder, and thereby to highlight natural capacity within human subjectivity and to marginalize the ability of divine grace to intrude upon an individual's life, those known as "antinomian" were more likely to fall into the opposite error of assuming that spiritual ends could never be achieved through physical or natural means, stressing the arbitrariness of divine initiative and consequent human passivity. Edwards railed against both movements and their theological underpinnings, and through his sermons, discourses, and miscellanies, promoted justification by grace, the righteousness of Christ, and the sovereign sanctifying work of the Spirit, which cumulatively allowed no room for either salvation *through* works or salvation *without* works, a summation of the Arminian and antinomian challenges respectively. Indeed, in the preface to the first edition of the *Faithful Narrative*, the British edi-

---

[32] E. Brooks Holifield, *The Covenant Sealed: The Development of Puritan Sacramental Theology in Old and New England, 1570–1720* (Eugene, OR: Wipf & Stock, 1974), 148.

tors (Isaac Watts and John Guyse) make clear that "such blessed instances of the success of the Gospel" (as are recounted there) have theological foundations that carefully navigate between such dangers:

> But wheresoever God works with power for salvation upon the minds of men, there will be some discoveries of a sense of sin, of the danger of the wrath of God, of the all-sufficiency of his Son Jesus, to relieve us under all our spiritual wants and distresses. . . . And if our readers had opportunity (as we have had) to peruse several of the sermons which were preached during this glorious season, we should find that it is the common plain Protestant doctrine of the Reformation, without stretching towards the Antinomians on the one side, or the Arminians on the other, that the Spirit of God has been pleased to honor with such illustrious success.[33]

The Arminian debate in particular had stalked Edwards for some years when the Valley revival (1734–1735) finally came. The rector of Yale, Timothy Cutler, and the tutors Samuel Johnson and Daniel Browne, had on October 16, 1722, declared their intention to join the Church of England associated in many minds with incipient Arminianism,[34] for which their employment at Yale was not surprisingly terminated.[35] As well, the Rand and Breck affairs were the focus of much energy and grief in Massachusetts in the early to mid-1730s. William Rand (1700–1779) and Robert Breck (1713–1784) were both Harvard graduates, whose apparently heterodox opinions had won them notoriety in Hampshire County, the former for instigating in Sunderland "the great noise which was in this part of the country about Arminianism,"[36] and the lat-

---

[33] "Faithful Narrative," *WJE*, 4:132.

[34] Anglicanism was particularly obnoxious to New England Puritans: "In ecclesiology the Puritans argued that congregational government was more biblical and less prone to corruption than prelacy. They also accused the Latitudinarian movement in Anglicanism of feeding the increased authority given to reason at Harvard. In Puritan vocabulary, Arminianism, Latitudinarianism, and Prelacy were synonymous with heresy, and Anglicanism possessed all three." George G. Levesque, "Quaestio: Peccator non Iustificatur Coram Deo Nisi per Iustitiam Christi Fide Apprehensam," *WJE*, 14:50n5.

[35] Wilson H. Kimnach, "Preface to the New York Period," in *WJE*, vol. 10, *Sermons and Discourses 1720–1723* (New Haven, CT: Yale University Press, 1992), 287.

[36] "Faithful Narrative," *WJE*, 14:148. Goen points out the false conclusion of Goodwin that the "great noise" referred to the Breck affair; in Goen's estimation, it was rather issues connected

ter for the "late lamentable Springfield contention."[37] Breck was to have accepted a ministerial settlement in Springfield, though his Arminian beliefs divided the congregation and caused unrest amongst local clergy before his eventual ordination on January 26, 1736. Though these cases may appear to be minor irritants rather than substantial causes, for Edwards they were quickly connected to the incident in Yale in 1722 when leading Congregationalists defected to Anglicanism, and reflected a broader change of mood, in which

> for at least half a century the whole basis of church life in New England had been shifting imperceptibly to human effort and moral striving, so that quite unawares many orthodox ministers were encouraging a subtle form of salvation by works. Indeed, this is what "Arminianism" meant in mid-eighteenth-century New England: it had less to do with Jacobus Arminius (1560–1609), the Dutch theologian from whom it took its name, than with a mood of rising confidence in man's ability to gain some purchase of the divine favor by human endeavor.[38]

Breck's ordination, upheld on appeal to the Massachusetts General Assembly, not only represented local threats to the traditional *theological* order, it also flagged for Edwards and those of his ministerial association the growing influence of the congregation, which had nominated and defended Breck, at the expense of the learned opinion of the clergy, who were resisting his appointment. The label "Arminian" implied a threat to the *ecclesiastical* order as well as to theological norms.[39]

These incidents are eloquent witness to the infiltration of Enlightenment ideas into New England, which had begun to cause deep anxiety: the possibility of Puritan life remaining hermetically sealed from the outside world appeared less and less ten-

---

to the ministry of William Rand in Sunderland which at this moment was so disturbing. See Clarence C. Goen, "Editor's Introduction," *WJE*, 4:9, 17–18; Gerald J. Goodwin, "'The Myth of 'Arminian-Calvinism' in Eighteenth-Century New England," *New England Quarterly* 41/2 (1968): 213–37, esp. 221.

[37] "Faithful Narrative," *WJE*, 4:145.

[38] Goen, "Editor's Introduction," *WJE*, 4:10.

[39] William J. Scheick, "Family, Conversion, and the Self in Jonathan Edwards' *A Faithful Narrative of the Surprising Work of God*," *Tennessee Studies in Literature* 18 (1973): 79–89.

able. The revocation by James II in 1684 of the Massachusetts Bay Charter, which had guaranteed Puritan social order, had shocked leading New England Puritans. The appointment of Joseph Dudley as acting governor of Massachusetts, New Hampshire, and Maine, and then Sir Edmund Andros as governor of the newly formed Dominion of New England in 1686, eliminated altogether the popular basis for government in the colonies, previously so highly prized. These developments were no doubt also partly a reaction to the anarchy of the English Civil War (1642–1651), of the Puritan Commonwealth (1649–1653), and of the Protectorate under Oliver Cromwell (1653–1659), all of which encouraged many Christians to long for a less chaotic and more settled Christian polity. This was finally achieved in the Restoration of the Stuart King Charles II in 1660. Indeed, in 1707 the very structure of English life itself changed with the birth of the unified Kingdom of Great Britain in the merging of the parliaments of Scotland and England.

These developments found their philosophical support in the rationalizing and ordering which the Newtonian system applied to both science and sociology. Though not driven to armed interventions in the New World, the Congregationalists somehow sensed the labile nature of their ecclesiological model, which was expressed in the desire by some for Presbyterian polity, and the increasing attraction of English mores and Episcopal structure. Together, there grew a greater tolerance of Anglican (and perhaps Arminian) conceptions of church and nation. These increasing attempts at imperial integration, even ecclesiastical Anglicization, of the colonies, and a kind of political centralization anathema to the Puritan cause, along with cautions concerning the New England Way, prepared the way for the Arminian challenge.

Edwards responded to the Arminians not just because their views were a threat to the Protestant priority of divine grace and human inability in salvation, focused in the doctrine of justification, but also because he saw, quite presciently, that these views together with the social realities that they represented, would undermine the nature of the local congregation and its delicate arrangement of spiritual responsibility between the monarchy of

Christ, the aristocracy of the elders, and the democratic contributions of the laity, as was espoused in the Cambridge Platform of 1648.[40] Authority would be dangerously relocated if the Arminian scheme made an appeal to an individual's self-determining will, within the context of the life and structure of the church, which gave no deference to other instituted ranks or received norms. Furthermore, such social autonomy would play into the hands of those economic libertines, who resisted any constraint being imposed on their mercantile aspirations on a frontier where the oversight of government was minimal.[41] It is significant that the Williams clan of western Massachusetts, who were later to prove so intransigent toward Edwards's reform of the practice of admission to the Lord's Supper, were ambitious for social aggrandizement and were ominously and tellingly aggrieved by his earlier sermons on justification in 1734–1735.[42]

Furthermore, Edwards demonstrates his antipathy toward the Arminian agenda when he defends not just the *content* of his preaching of justification as a significant factor in the Connecticut River revivals, but appeals as well to the *manner* with which he preached his sermons. Their significance on the frontier in Northampton was doubly efficacious. He suggests that the sermons which appear in *Discourses on Various Important Subjects* had value to his listeners from "the frame in which they heard them," and not so much because of "any real worth in them,"[43] perhaps as a Calvinist feigning modesty while disinclined to draw attention to his own skills and contributions.[44]

---

[40] Chapter 10 in "The Cambridge Platform" in *Creeds of the Churches: A Reader in Christian Doctrine from the Bible to the Present*, ed. J. H. Leith (Louisville, KY: John Knox, 1982), 393. It ought to be remembered as well that the vision of Puritan society saw the governing authority instituted to "restrain the selfishness of the individual for the sake of the commonwealth," not to encourage individual expression. See William G. McLoughlin, *Revivals, Awakenings, and Reform: An Essay on Religion and Social Change in America, 1607–1977*, Chicago History of American Religion (Chicago: University of Chicago Press, 1978), 79.

[41] Miller, *Jonathan Edwards*, 325. The nature of the will, later addressed by Edwards in a substantial discourse, was at issue between Arminianism and those defending Reformed principles. See Bogue, *Covenant of Grace*, 231.

[42] Cherry, *Theology*, 203.

[43] "Preface," *WJE*, 19:794.

[44] Philip F. Gura, *Jonathan Edwards: America's Evangelical* (New York: Hill & Wang, 2005), 75. The sermons' value to Northampton Christians was evident, for they were prepared to contribute financially toward their publication, even though the costs of the building of the new meeting-house in that year of 1738 were considerable.

Edwards is keen to distinguish himself from urban and urbane styles of Arminian preaching, when he describes his account of justification as "easy and plain." He reminds his readers that it is not so much aspiration toward *plainness of doctrine* that is noble, as aspiration toward *plainness of speech*. His opponents' defense in their "new-fashioned divinity" was to promote a "plain, easy and natural account of things,"[45] which eviscerated the substance of justification. Edwards readily acknowledges that making fine distinctions is at the heart of theological exposition in order to defend "the old Protestant doctrine of justification by faith alone," though the "Preface" provides a concentration of his arguments concerning the importance of clear homiletical style alongside cogent teaching:

> The practical discourses that follow have but little added to them, and now appear in that very plain and unpolished dress, in which they were first prepared and delivered; which was mostly at a time, when the circumstances of the auditory they were preached to, were enough to make a minister neglect, forget, and despise such ornaments as politeness, and modishness of style and method, when coming as a messenger from God to souls. . . . However unable I am to preach or write politely, if I would, yet I have this to comfort me under such a defect, that God has showed us he does not need such talents in men to carry on his own work, and that he has been pleased to smile upon and bless a very plain, unfashionable way of preaching.[46]

For Edwards, such a polemical commitment to unadorned use of language, even if it was true in design more than in delivery, was nevertheless a further marker of his position as authentic spokesman of God's Word to the plain people of the frontier, drawing on the traditional Puritan plain style of preaching. It was not just preaching the content of justification that prompted revival—it was the manner of preaching justification which set him apart from the stylized homiletics of the Arminian metropolis and

---

[45] "Preface," *WJE*, 19:795.
[46] Ibid., 19:797.

which was used of God.[47] That "remarkable season" of 1734–1735 attested both the victory of a theological *doctrine* and the social *dynamic* in which it found its home.

"This Town Has So Much Cause Ever to Remember": Justification Applied to Society

Truly, it was the town which benefitted from the preaching of justification expressed in renewed relationships: children, several families, households almost without exception, and "several Negroes . . . appear to have been truly born again in the late remarkable season,"[48] and, notably, antagonisms between minister and people were healed.[49] It is easy to imagine from a theological perspective that a revival comprised the assembling of regenerate individuals with their own distinct testimonies. From a philosophical perspective, in the Age of Enlightenment, it is tempting to read back into the individuality of those awakened a newfound autonomy and appreciation of individual experience, which reflected a paradigm shift in Western culture. It behooves us well therefore to pause and remind ourselves of the profoundly corporate mind-set and social location of Edwards, his audience, and those whom he opposed. As Ward so succinctly suggests: "The New England parish was more than a device for paying a minister; it was a social ideal."[50]

Edwards maintained that sponsoring the regeneration of individuals would not necessarily lead to the fissiparous disordering of the community, as some feared, but the moral transformation of the community as it rediscovered its corporate moorings and thereby its social vision.[51] McLoughlin reminds us that "[r]evitalization of the individual led to efforts to revitalize society. . . . Religious revivalism, saving souls, is in this respect a political activity, a way of producing a reborn majority to remodel society

---

[47] Wilson H. Kimnach, "Edwards as Preacher" in *The Cambridge Companion to Jonathan Edwards*, ed. S. J. Stein (Cambridge: University Press, 2007), 114.
[48] "Faithful Narrative," *WJE*, 4:158–59.
[49] Stout, *The New England Soul*, 188.
[50] W. Reginald Ward, *The Protestant Evangelical Awakening* (Cambridge: University Press, 1992), 277.
[51] Michael Crawford, *Seasons of Grace: Colonial New England's Revival Tradition in Its British Context* (New York: Oxford University Press, 1991), 15, 124, 189.

according to God's will and with his help."[52] In New England, revival was intricately linked to the renewal of the covenant, for the "assumption on which the concept of a revival of religion rests is that God deals with entire communities as discrete moral entities."[53] The social vision implicit in the earliest phases of revival is highlighted by Edwards in the *Faithful Narrative* of 1738:

> About this time, began the great noise that was in this part of the country about Arminianism, which seemed to appear with a very threatening aspect upon the interest of religion here. . . . Many who looked on themselves as in a Christless condition, seemed to be awakened by it, with fear that God was about to withdraw from the land, and that we should be given up to heterodoxy and corrupt principles. . . . This work of God, as it was carried on, and the number of true saints multiplied, soon made a glorious alteration in the town; so that in the spring and summer following, *anno* 1735, the town seemed to be full of the presence of God: it never was so full of love, nor so full of joy. . . . Our public assemblies were then beautiful.[54]

Gerald McDermott is of the view that Edwards works to reestablish social cohesion through his ministry, even if his new conception of society is based not on traditional static hierarchy but on a dynamic and relational experiential order.[55] Even if the locus of religious authority was repositioned to occupy the seat of the human heart, it could still be possible to build a social vision around democratic religious expression, rather than clerical control.[56]

This very issue constituted the Arminian threat to New England. On the one hand it was true that Arminianism represented a *liberating conception of human capacity* (which the preaching of justification sought to stymie). On the other, implicit

---

[52] McLoughlin, *Revivals, Awakenings, and Reform*, 75.
[53] Crawford, *Seasons of Grace*, 20. Crawford goes on to describe the ways in which New England differed from the Middle Colonies with its assumptions of "the outpouring of grace for the transformation of a community." Ibid., 122–23, 247.
[54] "Faithful Narrative," *WJE*, 4:148, 151.
[55] Gerald R. McDermott, *One Holy and Happy Society: The Public Theology of Jonathan Edwards* (University Park, PA: Pennsylvania State University Press, 1992), 137, 141.
[56] Ibid., 153–54.

Arminian appeal to a new conception of order and stability based on education, morality, and moderation served to reinforce *a social vision of hierarchy and elitism* more radical than local congregationalism had ever known.[57] The enthusiasm of the revivals reminded many of the causes and consequences of disruptive Puritan polity in seventeenth-century Old England, so the reaction of Arminians was to appeal to the rationality and security of a more recent status quo. Charles Chauncy, the leading Boston preacher of his day, was opposed to the revivals for this very reason. His argument was that revivalist preaching appealed to the will rather than to the mind, and in consequence was socially dangerous:

> Chauncy represented an extreme aspect of the intellectualist tradition that emphasized the "understanding" and strict clerical control over congregations. Edwards spoke for the voluntarist tradition that emphasized the "affections" and favoured more active lay involvement in church affairs. . . . As long as the sources of true enthusiasm lay within the grasp of natural man, then the true enthusiast was the person of superior breeding and refined sensibilities. But if the source of true enthusiasm came from without—as Edwards insisted it did—then *anyone* was a potential candidate for remaking, and distinctions of learning or breeding lost their significance. . . . In a theological sense Edwards had simply reclothed the old Calvinist teachings of sin and grace in a new rhetoric of sentiment. But in a social sense he accomplished far more: he cut a doorway to an assertive lay piety that would open far wider than he ever imagined and that would permanently alter the relations between pastors and congregations in more democratic directions.[58]

Both Chauncy and Edwards would have cause to speak out as well against antinomianism due to its potential for destabilization, though their own preferred social vision was at variance. The renegotiation of ministry structures provoked by the revivals and the growth of itinerancy fell to both sides of the debate:

---

[57] McLoughlin, *Revivals, Awakenings, and Reform*, 71–72.
[58] Stout, *The New England Soul*, 203, 207.

> Both Arminian and Reformed opposers worried that by appearing to divorce the knowledge of a person's conversion from her or his outward behavior, the doctrine of inward assurance undermined Christianity's role in the preservation of that person's place and the place of every other person within the deferential, elite-brokered social order.[59]

While Edwards had a greater capacity to tolerate dynamic social relations than Chauncy, he nevertheless would draw a line against separatism, or the disposition that encouraged "spiritual individualism." It was understood that both Arminianism and antinomianism were essentially "egocentric" and thereby socially unstable.[60]

Furthermore, for Edwards to preach justification as a strategy to hold together the disruptive initiative of God toward the individual alongside the dynamic yet ultimately orderly intentions of God toward the community, was to redefine the role of the minister in his own social setting. He may act as midwife in the birth of new spiritual life in a local church or town, but it could not be assumed that the resulting spiritual enthusiasm could be constrained through clerical control. The minister's responsibilities were still well-defined, even if his authority was mediated through the influence of charismatic gifting rather than office.[61] In Edwards's *Farewell Sermon*, preached at Northampton in June 22, 1750, after the decision was taken to dismiss him from his position there, he effectively locates his own ministry as a continuance of the ministry of the prophets and apostles as divine ambassador to the people. He identified himself with the prophet Jeremiah, who had similarly preached for twenty-three years with little fruit for his labors, and Edwards uses the text of 2 Corinthians 1:14 to demonstrate his authority as a messenger from God, even if the local congregation renounced his minis-

---

[59] Timothy D. Hall, *Contested Boundaries: Itinerancy and the Reshaping of the Colonial American Religious World* (Durham, NC: Duke University Press, 1994), 54.
[60] Heimert, *Religion and the American Mind*, 129.
[61] E. Brooks Holifield, *God's Ambassadors: A History of the Christian Clergy in America*, Pulpit & Pew, (Grand Rapids, MI: Eerdmans, 2007), 69. Edwards is unusual amongst the revivalists of the middle of the eighteenth century in as far as he preached for revival as a settled pastor and not as an itinerant.

trations.[62] Preaching justification had been for Edwards a burdensome responsibility with patchy and painful results. Unlike the clerical preparationists, who micromanaged the advance of grace in individuals' lives with paternalistic oversight, Edwards stood apart from the flock, literally in the end, and gave priority to prophetic rather than pastoral concerns as he called the people toward a renewed commitment to the community of grace.[63] Justification came to be associated with a divisive social strategy as much as divine and saving balm.

Janice Knight elaborates further on Edwards's self-identification as prophet, which functioned as a foil to both Arminian and antinomian threats to the New England project, for while Edwards avoids righteousness through works and righteousness through spontaneous spiritual illumination, he nevertheless defends the prospect of a broadly conceived social righteousness as a result of transformed lives. Edwards's belief that local revivals constitute an essential part of the divine purpose to win the world for Christ ultimately situates his ministry within a regional, or perhaps *international*, movement, and relativizes the pastor's responsibility within the *local* church. The revivals are themselves germane to an eschatological vision for the world:

> Edwards watched and worked for the advent of the Kingdom. He believed that increasing the numbers of the faithful was instrumental in bringing forth those glorious days. Exhortations to the saints, unions in prayer, and efforts at international alliances with other churches were some of the ways Edwards labored to knit the churches and bring forth the Kingdom.[64]

Edwards's preaching of justification does not depend on a mechanical sequence of "steps to the altar," as present in traditional New

---

[62] Jonathan Edwards, "A Farewell Sermon Preached at the First Precinct in Northampton, after the People's Public Rejection of Their Minister . . . on June 22, 1750," in *WJE*, vol. 25, *Sermons and Discourses 1743–1758*, ed. W. H. Kimnach (New Haven, CT: Yale University Press, 2006), 475, 485.
[63] Hall provides an overview of the themes of pastor and prophet in conceptions of ministry in the New World. See David D. Hall, *The Faithful Shepherd: A History of New England Ministry in the Seventeenth Century* (Chapel Hill, NC: University of North Carolina Press, 1972), 49, for an opening definition.
[64] Janice Knight, *Orthodoxies in Massachusetts: Rereading American Puritanism* (Cambridge, MA: Harvard University Press, 1994), 208.

England preparationism. Nor does Edwards's understanding of justification merely address the individuated need of immediate spiritual experience and assurance of sins forgiven, as would befit a defensive and contractual legal exchange without any reference to the community of faith. Rather, Edwards's approach to the doctrine of justification by grace through faith situates it as an outworking of divine initiative and generosity, which cannot be artificially contained within the local setting but spills over to transform the world.[65] Unlike Stoddard who saw no discernible pattern, for Edwards the revivals were harbingers of hope, with not just national but international scope.[66] Edwards did not believe that New England's privileges were inviolable; his prophetic ministry would not allow him merely to affirm New England's "glorious" past. He was however optimistic, for though the revivals may force acknowledgment of the distinction between the regenerate and the damned in New England churches, such division was not an end in itself, but would provide an impetus to formulate an alternative model of ministry and expectation of blessing for the ends of the earth.[67]

Conclusion: The Gospel Edwards Preached

For a conservative thinker within the Reformed tradition, it may seem churlish to ask questions concerning the gospel that Edwards preached. He was assuredly Christocentric and supernaturalist, and as this chapter has explained, Edwards understood the doctrine of justification as the tipping point in his revivalist program. He preached other doctrinal loci, but none seemed to encapsulate his theological, philosophical, and transformational agenda more effectively. It is often assumed that Edwards's gospel was highly subjectivist, growing out of his commitment to religious affections, which were the location of true religion,[68] and that to preach the gospel was merely to preach an individual

[65] Ibid., 1–4.
[66] Crawford, *Seasons of Grace*, 134.
[67] McDermott, *One Holy and Happy Society*, 34.
[68] Jonathan Edwards, *The Works of Jonathan Edwards*, vol. 2, *Religious Affections*, ed. John E. Smith (New Haven, CT: Yale University Press, 1969), 95.

experience of salvation from sin, or salvation from God's wrath as sin's consequence. William Abraham asserts with reference to Edwards that this "anthropocentric turn has been the undoing of modern evangelism."[69]

However, Edwards's gospel was not an attenuated theory of atonement, nor could it be summarized as the good news of an experience of rebirth. His gospel was neither an idea without application, nor an experience without foundation. For Edwards, the assumptions of covenant life in New England, the millennial frame of his ministry, and his prophetic self-understanding position his preaching of justification as more than an appeal to decision, but as shorthand for *forgiveness, favor,* and *international fellowship* in the coming kingdom. He preached for repentance, but this was as much a call to eschatological expectation as it was to spiritual renewal. Here was simply no *revivalist evangelicalism,* but rather Edwards was the fountainhead of a *confessional evangelicalism* with sweeping vision, which nevertheless included as significant features passion and preaching and prayer for revivals in every land.

Edwards's gospel is necessarily social in its outworkings. The gospel is power for salvation, but it is a power expressed (in the thought-world of Paul) in the incorporation of both Jew and Gentile into the church of God (Rom. 1:16; Eph. 2:11–18). There was an *imperative* in the gospel which Edwards preached, calling on his listeners to exercise faith, that the righteousness of God might avail to them (Rom. 1:17), but unlike much revivalism after him, he did not sideline the *indicative* of God's eternal power and divine nature (Rom. 1:20), or God's revelation of righteousness and wrath (Rom. 1:17–18), or the role of the law in our condemnation (Rom. 3:19).[70] Other revivalists may have minimized the content of the indicative, or left it out altogether, but Edwards is clear that there is neither personal revival, nor indeed social reform,

---

[69] William Abraham, *The Logic of Evangelism* (Grand Rapids, MI: Eerdmans, 1989), 58.
[70] With reference to the sermon "The Justice of God in the Damnation of Sinners," Logan helpfully draws our attention to the minimal amount of material "urging a decision upon his people." Logan, "The Northampton Revival," 252, 258. For the text of the sermon: Jonathan Edwards, "The Justice of God in the Damnation of Sinners," *WJE,* 19:esp. 348ff.

without doctrinal revelation, which itself constitutes the primacy of ecclesial identity.[71] It is not that Edwards only expressed the gospel in terms of God's righteousness, justice, or justification, but that this nevertheless became for him a significant theological instrument in a sociological context that needed drastic restorative attention. His gospel of justification applied to a panoply of ailments was a powerful antidote, certainly individual yet also confidently social.

---

[71] Ian Stackhouse, "Revivalism, Faddism and the Gospel," in *On Revival: A Critical Examination*, eds. A. Walker and K. Aune (Carlisle, PA: Paternoster Press, 2003), 244.

Chapter Four

Justification and Evangelical Obedience

Samuel T. Logan Jr.

"What makes a person a Christian?"

Understood correctly, this question captures the heart of the centuries-long historical debate about the relationship between justification and sanctification.

Understood correctly, this question captures the spirit of the contemporary debate between those whom Jim Belcher, in his book *Deep Church*, calls "traditionalists" on the one hand and "emergents" on the other.[1]

And understood correctly, this question captures the essence of what Edwards was seeking to express in his theology.

"What makes a person a Christian?" should be understood and appreciated in at least these two syntactical senses: (1) What ontologically causes a person to become a Christian? and (2) How is a person recognized as being a Christian?

With regard to the first of these two senses, what is it that moves a person "from spiritual death to spiritual life"? What moves him/her from being a member of the kingdom of darkness/man to being a member of the kingdom of light/God? Or, to frame the question in the terms that most interested Edwards, who gets the "credit" for the change? The question is not about influences or contexts or missions or evangelism; it is about the specific power which causes the change. Most fundamentally, the

---

[1] Jim Belcher, *Deep Church: A Third Way Beyond Emerging and Traditional* (Downers Grove, IL: IVP, 2010, Kindle edition, see esp. locations 930–1310.

question is this: "Does man cause the change or does God cause the change?"

With regard to the second of the above-mentioned senses of our question, what are the "signs" that a person is a Christian? What must characterize any genuine Christian? Or, to frame the question in the terms that most interested Edwards, for what should a church look when considering a person for full communicant membership (and on what should church judicatories insist in selecting its leaders)? The question here is not solely about what a person thinks or about how a person acts, although these are extraordinarily important markers. Most fundamentally, the question is this: "Is God or is man the focus of this person's life?"

Of course, implications abound from both senses of the question, and Edwards's sermons and treatises trace out all manner of such implications, both theoretical and practical. But fundamentally, the issue really is this: what makes a person a Christian?

Historical Context

The very first major theological dispute in New England, involving Anne Hutchinson and John Cotton, embodies elements of this question. The Puritan "errand into the wilderness" was not primarily a search for religious freedom, though it is often portrayed as such. Reading the journal of John Winthrop, the first and frequently reelected governor of the colony, makes it clear that the purpose of the Massachusetts Bay Colony was to be an example of holiness, a "Modell of Christian Charity," so that England, the home that many of those Puritans had reluctantly left, would repent and be healed.[2]

In order to assure the holiness of that example, the leaders of the Massachusetts Bay Colony took two separate but critically interconnected actions—they restricted the franchise (the vote) to members in good standing of Puritan churches in the Colony and they instituted a "visible saints" criterion for membership

---

[2] John Winthrop, "A Modell of Christian Charity," in *Sermons That Shaped America*, eds. William S. Barker and Samuel T. Logan (Phillipsburg, NJ: P&R, 2003), 23–36.

in those churches.[3] The details of these actions have been studied and debated for decades but, for our purposes here, it needs
simply to be noted that, from its earliest years, identification of
"what makes a person a Christian" was of utmost importance in
the Massachusetts Bay Colony.

And it wasn't long before varying answers to that question
threatened completely to scuttle the "errand into the wilderness."
To state the problem in simple and stark terms, was it external
behavior or was it internal status which the church and the state
should examine most carefully in determining whether a person
was *really* a Christian (and could therefore take communion in the
church and vote in civil elections)? The theological dispute mentioned above arose when Anne Hutchinson heard her minister,
John Cotton, to be emphasizing especially strongly the internal
working of the Holy Spirit and began to teach the same to others.
Out of her teaching emerged what historians now call "the antinomian controversy."[4]

This chapter, however, is not about either Anne Hutchinson
or John Cotton. It is about Jonathan Edwards. Where is the exact
link between Hutchinson/Cotton and Edwards? That link is provided by one of the Massachusetts ministers directly involved
in the dispute in Boston in the 1630s, the Rev. Thomas Shepard.
Shepard was one of the Boston ministers most concerned about
what Cotton was reported to have said and the exchange of let-
ters between Shepard and Cotton reveals the depth of suspicion
between the two.[5]

At least partly as a result of his concern about the ramifications of what he understood Cotton to be teaching, Shepard
preached a series of sermons on "The Parable to the Ten Virgins,"
which were published in 1659 after Shepard's death. These sermons contained Shepard's attempt to answer the question, what

---

[3] See Edmund Morgan's analyses of these actions in *Visible Saints: The History of a Puritan Idea*
(Ithaca, NY: Cornell University Press, 1963) and in *The Puritan Dilemma: The Story of John Winthrop*
(Boston: Little, Brown, 1958). See also Winthrop in *Sermons*, 18–23.
[4] Morgan, *Dilemma*, 134–53. Most of the relevant primary source documents relating to this
"controversy" may be found in David Hall, *The Antinomina Controversy, 1636–1638* (Durham, NC:
Duke University Press, 1990).
[5] Hall, *Antinomina Controversy*, 24–33.

makes a person a Christian? In the terms of the parable on which Shepard focused his attention, how exactly do we recognize "wise virgins," that is, those who are genuinely prepared for the return of the Master? And the importance of this material for the present study can be seen in the fact that, other than the Bible, Edwards quotes more from Shepard's material than from any other in his *Treatise on Religious Affections*, which is Edwards's most profound answer to the question, what makes a person a Christian?[6]

Edwards's Sermons on Justification

But the broad scope of American theological history is not the only context out of which Edwards developed his answer to this crucial question. There was a more immediate context as well.

In the fall of 1734, writes Edwards in his introduction to *A Faithful Narrative of the Surprising Work of God*, "began the great noise in this part of the country, about Arminianism, which seemed to appear with a very threatening aspect upon the interest of religion here."[7] Edwards then goes on to add that, because of this "noise," "There were some things said publicly on that occasion, concerning justification by faith alone."[8] Those "things said publicly" were, in fact, Edwards's own sermons that were later collected into what we now regard as Edwards's treatise on justification by faith alone.

Edwards's justification treatise has (appropriately) received extensive attention, and I will not try here to deal with all of its intricacies. I do, however, want to summarize a couple of the salient points before moving on to what I regard as Edwards's most mature expression of his answer to the question, what makes a person a Christian?

Edwards preached these sermons, as indicated above, in response to what he regarded as "Arminian noises" in Western

---

[6] John E. Smith, "Editor's Introduction" to "The Treatise on Religious Affections" in *The Works of Jonathan Edwards* (hereafter WJE), vol. 2, *Religious Affections*, ed. John E. Smith (New Haven, CT: Yale University Press, 1959), 53–57.

[7] Samuel T. Logan Jr., "The Doctrine of Justification in the Theology of Jonathan Edwards," *Westminster Theological Journal* 46 (1984): 26ff.

[8] Ibid., 26.

Massachusetts. In other words, Edwards saw a critical connection between Arminianism and the doctrine of justification by faith alone. He therefore used Romans 4:5 as the basis for the published form of these sermons: "And to the one who does not work but believes in him who justifies the ungodly, his faith is counted as righteousness." For Edwards, the key phrase in this verse was "who justifies the ungodly." And he spent a great deal of time examining the theological import of the fact that it is the *ungodly* whom God justifies. In other words, there is nothing whatsoever in the person whom God justifies that merits or causes that justification.

As he traces out all that this means, Edwards focuses his attention on two different things he understood Arminians to be claiming were at least part of what God considers when he grants justification to an individual—faith and evangelical obedience. Interestingly, these were two areas frequently cited as grounds on which individuals might be recognized as "visible saints" in the early days of the Massachusetts Bay Colony.[9]

Edwards has no doubt that both faith and obedience are critically important in the lives of those whom God redeems, but he also has no doubt that neither of these *causes* justification. And that is exactly how he builds his response to those noisy Arminians, by distinguishing between "cause" and "condition."

Two statements by Edwards communicate powerfully how he understands these different words. The word "cause," Edwards argues, is accurately used only

> to signify any *antecedent*, either natural or moral, positive or negative, on which an Event, either a thing, or the manner and circumstance of a thing, so depends, that it is the ground and reason, either in whole or in part, why it is, rather than not; or why it is as it is, rather than otherwise; or, in other words, any antecedent with which a consequent Event is so connected, that

---

[9] A set of transcriptions of actual "narratives of grace" given by successful church membership candidates is provided in Bruce Chapman Woolley, *Reverend Thomas Shepard's Cambridge Church Members, 1636–1649* (PhD diss., The University of Rochester, 1973).

it truly belongs to the reason why the proposition which affirms that Event is true; whether it has any positive influence, or not."[10]

On the other hand,

by the word condition, as it is very often (and perhaps most commonly) used, we mean anything that may have the place of a condition in a conditional proposition, and as such is truly connected with the consequent, especially if the proposition holds both in the affirmative and negative, as the condition is either affirmed or denied. If it be that with which, or which being supposed, a thing shall be, and without which, or it being denied, a thing shall not be, we in such a case call it a condition of that thing. . . . In one sense, Christ alone performs the condition of our justification and salvation; in another sense, other qualifications and acts are conditions of salvation and justification too. . . . There is a difference between being justified by a thing, and that thing universally, necessarily, and inseparably attending justification; for so do a great many things that we are not said to be justified by.[11]

In other words, there is only one *cause* of justification and that is the sovereign grace of God. But there are numerous *conditions* of justification, including faith and evangelical obedience. To be sure, Edwards, as a spiritual heir of Luther and Calvin, spends a great deal of time and exegetical energy distinguishing between faith and all of the other conditions of justification. It is faith alone by which the individual is united to Christ, a position that echoes John Calvin and presages John Murray.[12] Nevertheless, God alone is the One who *causes* the justification of any individual. Therefore, there is one and only one true answer to the first sense of our question—what is it that ontologically causes a person to become a Christian? That answer is God, and it was with that

---

[10] Jonathan Edwards, "Freedom of the Will," in *WJE*, ed. Edward Hickman, 2 vols. (1834; repr., Carlisle, PA: Banner of Truth, 1974), Kindle ed., 2010, locations 13558–13571.

[11] Jonathan Edwards, "Justification by Faith Alone" in *WJE*, vol. 1, Kindle ed., locations 54571–54597.

[12] Ibid., locations 54693–54706. See also John Calvin, *Institutes of the Christian Religion*, 2 vols., ed. John T. McNeill, trans. Ford Lewis Battles (Philadelphia: Westminster Press, 1960), 1:569–71, and John Murray, *Redemption Accomplished and Applied* (Grand Rapids, MI: Eerdmans, 1955), 161–73.

answer that Edwards sought to quiet the "noise of Arminianism" in Western Massachusetts in the mid 1730s.

Edwards's Mature Position

But while this answer may have seemed adequate to Edwards in 1734 and 1735, events during the next decade led him to realize that more—much more—needed to be said. More needed to be said because, for one thing, the Christian church in New England, between 1735 and 1745, experienced revival and awakening on an unprecedented scale. The church as a whole and individual churches went through extraordinary spiritual upheaval during that decade, the likes of which it remains difficult to discover in any other similar period in our nation's history.[13]

The primary occasion for the upheaval was the Great Awakening, a series of revivals that swept the colonies in what was probably the first "national event" in America's history. From Maine to Georgia, preachers saw hundreds, even thousands, of people professing faith in Jesus Christ, testifying that they had become Christians. On one occasion in October of 1742, the evangelist George Whitefield is said to have preached to a crowd of thirty thousand on the Boston Common, and at that time, Boston, the largest city in the colonies, had a total population of only ten thousand!

But as so often happens during periods of spiritual intensity, reports of the experiences of those impacted by the Awakening became more and more extreme as the years passed, and this made the identification of "genuinely gracious" experiences increasingly difficult and increasingly important. Edwards himself participated both in the preaching out of which arose such experiences and in the written description and evaluation of those experiences. One

---

[13] I am not sure that those of us who talk about the great spiritual changes taking place "in our day" fully appreciate the magnitude of some of the spiritual changes that occurred in earlier days. Christopher Hill (*The World Turned Upside Down* [London: Temple Smith, 1972]) presents a strong case that the 1640s in England was the most crucial decade in determining the religious and political shape of the modern Anglo-American world, and Bernard Bailyn, author of *The Ideological Origins of the American Revolution* (Cambridge, MA: Harvard University Press, 1967), (which won both the Pulitzer and the Bancroft Prizes) makes a similarly powerful case about the period between 1740 and 1776 in the American colonies. Historical perspective almost always moderates claims about the present.

of the most enlightening enterprises in Edwardsean scholarship is
to trace the gradual changes that took place in Edwards's response
to what happened in the churches of New England between 1735
and 1745, and those changes have everything to do with "what
makes a person a Christian."

Edwards's first direct examination of awakening phenomena
was his *Narrative of Surprising Conversions*, published in 1737. In
this work, Edwards enthusiastically, and almost without qualification, endorses the events he describes as clear manifestations
of the blessing of the Holy Spirit on his church. Indeed, in the
prefatory letter that is often attached to the *Narrative*, Edwards
cites the apparently miraculous intervention of the Holy Spirit
when the old Northampton church building collapsed (and *no
one* was injured!) as at least partial ground for his conviction
that the events he was about to describe were genuinely of the
Lord.[14] If this extraordinary physical and visible event occurred,
Edwards seems to be suggesting, there can be no question that
the events he was about to describe were genuinely manifestations of saving grace.

Throughout the *Narrative*, Edwards maintains this stance. He
constantly cites external and visible "proofs" for the reality and
the genuineness of the revival in Northampton. He talks at length
about the many places where revival occurred—South Hadley,
Suffield, Sunderland, Deerfield, Hatfield, West Springfield, Long
Meadow, Enfield, Northfield, Ripton, Newhaven, Guildford,
Mansfield, Tolland, Hebron, Bolton, Preston, Woodbury—and
even "the Jerseys."[15] He describes the way in which those touched
by the revival often find "scriptures one after another coming to
their minds to answer their scruples" (a particularly important
"sign" in light of what he says later in *The Affections*).

Perhaps the best-known sections of the *Narrative* describe the
experiences of Abigail Hutchinson and Phebe Bartlet. In the latter
case particularly, Edwards seems to focus quite directly on what
would be considered the external evidences of the work of the

---

[14] "Preface to *A Faithful Narrative*," *WJE*, vol. 1, Kindle ed., locations 36402–36427.
[15] "Faithful Narrative," *WJE*, vol. 1, Kindle ed., locations 36620–36645.

Spirit of God—attendance at Sunday worship, expressed appreciation for Edwards's own preaching, "bowells of compassion to the
poor," and "great love to her minister." Without doubt, the stories
about Abigail and Phebe communicate that, if the experiences are
unusual—either in the extreme peace shown in death (Abigail) or
in the extreme youth of the experiencer (Phebe)—one can almost
be assured that the experiences are genuine.

To be sure, in the *Narrative*, Edwards takes note of a few of
the ways in which not everything that appears genuine actually
is, but the overall impression left by this first reflection on the
revivals is that "what makes a person a Christian" can be seen and
measured fairly directly. No question—the *cause* of these events
must have been and can only have been the Spirit of God; Edwards
is unquestionably true to the conclusions of *Justification by Faith
Alone*. But external evidences, particularly unusual external evidences, are the primary way in which it is known that the Spirit
has been at work. Anne Hutchinson (and probably John Cotton)
would have been displeased—and Thomas Shepard would, at the
very least, have been uncertain.

In fact, Edwards himself, when reflecting on the *Narrative*, saw
serious deficiencies in it. Writing in his journal in 1750, Edwards
interprets his dismissal from the Northampton pulpit this way:

> One thing that has contributed to bring things to such a pass at
> Northampton, was my youth, and want of more judgment and
> experience, in the time of that extraordinary awakening, about
> sixteen years ago. Instead of a youth, there was want of a giant, in
> judgment and discretion, among a people in such an extraordi-
> nary state of things. In some respects, doubtless, my confidence
> in myself was a great injury to me; but in other respects, my dif-
> fidence of myself injured me. It was such that I durst not act my
> own judgment, and had no strength to oppose received notions,
> and established customs, and to testify boldly against some glar-
> ing false appearances, and counterfeits of religion, till it was too
> late. And by this means, as well as others, many things got foot-
> ing, which have proved a dreadful source of spiritual pride, and
> other things that are exceedingly contrary to true Christianity.
> If I had had more experience, and ripeness of judgment and

courage, I should have guided my people in a better manner, and should have guarded them better from Satan's devices, and prevented the spiritual calamity of many souls, and perhaps the eternal ruin of some of them; and have done what would have tended to lengthen out the tranquility of the town.[16]

It is absolutely critical that we hear what Edwards is saying here. He is *not* saying that his *theology* was deficient in 1734–1735. He is *not* saying that he had allowed Arminianism (or Pelagianism or Roman Catholicism) to invade his interpretation of the justifying works that the Spirit had done in Northampton during those years. There was never any question that Edwards had, in 1734–1736, compromised his belief that "God" is the ultimate and only ontological answer to the question, what makes a person a Christian? If there had been a problem at all, and clearly Edwards thinks that there was, it was located in how he answered the "recognition" sense of that question.

Further, his use, in 1750, of the word "counterfeit" suggests simply but clearly the way in which he had resolved the core issue in the intervening years.[17] To examine that resolution in detail, we need to move on through the next several pieces in which Edwards worked through the various issues relating to the issue of justification, the issue of what makes a person a Christian.

On September 10, 1741, Edwards preached the commencement sermon at Yale. The full title of that sermon was *The Distinguishing Marks of a Work of the Spirit of God, Applied to That Uncommon Operation That Has Lately Appeared on the Minds of Many of the People of New England, with a Particular Consideration of the Extraordinary Circumstances with Which This Work Is Attended*. Historical evidence suggests that the treatise form of this sermon appeared early in 1742, slightly before Edwards's next attempt to address the issues. That next attempt was *Some Thoughts Concerning the Present Revival of Religion in New England and the Way in Which It Ought to Be*

---

[16] "Memoirs of Jonathan Edwards," WJE, vol. 1, Kindle ed., locations 6709–6722.
[17] See Edwards's use of the word "counterfeit" at the beginning of "Distinguishing Marks," WJE, vol. 2, Kindle ed., locations 17615–17628.

Acknowledged and Promoted, Humbly Offered to the Public, in a Treatise on That Subject.[18]

Of course, both of these works had as their direct focus the events that we now call "the Great Awakening," rather than the events of the 1734–1735 revival, but the core issues of the two sets of events were the same. Granting that God and God alone *causes* a person's justification, what is the essential existential nature of that event in the life of the newly justified person? By 1742, this had become an incredibly important question because it had to do both with what the church (and its ministers) sought to be and to do and with how membership in the church was to be defined. We must remember that the early 1740s were exactly the years during which Edwards seems to have begun seriously to doubt the church membership policy of his grandfather, Solomon Stoddard, Edwards's predecessor at the Northampton church. And we also need to remember that the words (quoted above) that Edwards wrote in 1750 were written in the context of his being dismissed from his Northampton pastorate, a dismissal that might never have occurred if Edwards had not come to his conclusion about the full meaning of justification. The doctrine of justification is not, therefore, simply a matter of abstract theology. The doctrine of justification is directly involved in the definition of the nature and the purpose of the church.

So what did Edwards say in *Distinguishing Marks* and in *Thoughts on the Revival*? A good way to begin answering that question is to mention the overall structure of *Thoughts*. While in the *Narrative* Edwards largely endorses the events of 1734–1735, by the time of *Thoughts*, the balance has clearly shifted. *Thoughts* contain five distinct parts. In part 1 Edwards provides a defense of the Great Awakening as a work of God; in part 2 he offers a series of reasons why the Awakening should be supported even though problems have arisen; in part 3 he defends the promoters

---

[18] See the brief but excellent discussion of Edwards's position in Mark Shaw, *Global Awakening: How 20th-Century Revivals Triggered a Christian Revolution* (Downers Grove, IL: InterVarsity Press, 2010), 20–21. Shaw does an especially good job linking the past to the present and thus demonstrating the relevance of church history to modern ministry.

of the Awakening against attacks that have been made on them; in part 4 he lists and discusses the very real dangers that have arisen from within the Awakening; and in part 5 he suggests ways of promoting the Awakening. This makes it seem as though Edwards is still largely supportive of the Awakening, and, in some ways, he is. But the critical and defining fact is that part 4, where he catalogs the dangers inherent in the Awakening, is by far the longest section and makes up about 40 percent of the entire treatise.

What are those dangers and how do they relate to our ongoing question, what makes a person a Christian? The key concept here, as it was in the passage quoted earlier and as it will be when we come to the *Religious Affections*, is best captured by the word "counterfeit." Hear Edwards as he begins part 4 of *Thoughts*: "If we look back into the history of the church of God in past ages, we may observe that it has been a common device of the devil, to overset a revival of religion; when he finds that he can keep men quiet and secure no longer, then he drives them to excesses and extravagances."[19]

Many of us, in our understanding of what happened during the Awakening, may immediately conclude that Edwards is talking about extremely emotional religious displays—and, of course, he is. But he is talking about much more than that. He is concerned with those, both in his day and ours, who would regard themselves as among the most vigorous proponents of the orthodox Reformed doctrine of justification, as among those who maintain most clearly and vehemently the truth that God and God alone is the causal answer to the ontological question, what makes a person a Christian?

One clue that Edwards has more than extreme emotion in mind is the passage which immediately precedes the one quoted above. Speaking directly and specifically about the man whom many regard as having recaptured the orthodox doctrine of justification, Edwards says this: "Luther, the head of the reformation,

---

[19] "Thoughts on the Revival," *WJE*, vol. 1, Kindle ed., locations 39753–39765.

who was guilty of a great many excesses in that great affair in which God made him the chief instrument . . . "[20]

What in the world might Edwards have in mind here? As he begins his actual enumeration of the main errors that have appeared in those who supported and promoted the Awakening, he says:

> The first and worse cause of errors, that prevail in such a state of things, is spiritual pride. This is the main door by which the devil comes into the hearts of those who are zealous for the advancement of religion. It is the chief inlet of smoke from the bottomless pit, to darken the mind and mislead the judgment. This is the main handle by which the devil has hold of religious persons, and the chief source of all the mischief that he introduces, to clog and hinder a work of God. This cause of error is the main spring, or at least the main support, of all the rest. Till this disease is cured, medicines are in vain applied to heal other diseases. It is by this that the mind defends itself in other errors, and guards itself against light, by which it might be corrected and reclaimed. The spiritually proud man is full of light already, he does not need instruction, and is ready to despise the offer of it. But if this disease is healed, other things are easily rectified.[21]

Edwards does not, of course, downgrade or diminish in any way the seriousness of the error of those who define justification in an Arminian or Pelagian manner. If 38 percent of *Thoughts* is made up of his discussion of the errors of the Awakening's supporters, this means that 62 percent could be said to be made up of his discussion of the errors of those who oppose the Awakening. God and God alone causes justification. God and God alone is the answer to the ontological question, what makes a person a Christian?

But Edwards could not be clearer in *Thoughts*—the greatest hindrance to the work of the gospel does not come from those who make the Arminian error about justification. The greatest hindrance to the work of the gospel comes from those whose theological belief systems may be absolutely correct, whose under-

---

[20] Ibid., locations 39753–39759.
[21] Ibid., locations 39828–39840.

standing of the theology of justification is right on target, but whose Christian lives communicate what Edwards in other places calls "censoriousness." Here is what he says under the heading, "Some particular errors that have risen from several of the preceding causes—Censuring others":

> And here the first thing I would take notice of, is censuring professing Christians of good standing in the visible church, as unconverted. I need not repeat what I have elsewhere said to show this to be against the plain, frequent, and strict prohibitions of the word of God. It is the worst disease that has attended this work, and most contrary to the spirit and rules of Christianity, and of the worst consequences.[22]

Another aspect of this kind of error is what Edwards calls "separatism":

> Spiritual pride disposes persons to affect separation, to stand at a distance from others, as being better than they; and loves the show and the appearance of the distinction. But, on the contrary, the eminently humble Christian is ready to look upon himself as not worthy that others should be united to him—to think himself more brutish than any man, and worthy to be cast out of human society—and especially unworthy of the society of God's children. And though he will not be a companion with one that is visibly Christ's enemy, . . . yet he does not love the appearance of an open separation from visible Christians.[23]

These are all Edwards's descriptions of those who would agree with him that God and God alone causes justification but who somehow have missed at least one critically important aspect of the truth about "what makes a person a Christian." That aspect is the primary focus of Edwards's most important work, *A Treatise Concerning Religious Affections.*

Published in 1746, the same year in which the college that Edwards would lead briefly in the last year of his life was founded, *The Affections* builds extensively on what Edwards had said in

---

[22] Ibid., locations 40858–40876.
[23] Ibid., locations 39952–39982.

Distinguishing Marks. As in the earlier work, Edwards begins by identifying the most serious problem facing the Christian church as "counterfeit Christianity":

> It is by the mixture of counterfeit religion with true, not discerned and distinguished, that the devil has had his greatest advantage against the cause and kingdom of Christ. It is plainly by this means, principally, that he has prevailed against all revivals of religion, since the first founding of the Christian church.[24]

Edwards then sets himself the task, in this his most significant work, of separating the genuine from the counterfeit: "Therefore, it greatly concerns us to use our utmost endeavors, clearly to discern, and have it well settled and established, wherein true religion does consist. . . . What I aim at now, is to show the nature and signs of the gracious operations of God's Spirit, by which they are to be distinguished from all things whatsoever which are not of a saving nature."[25]

By framing the issue as he does, Edwards asserts a vitally important principle: the *nature* of the operations of God's Spirit and the *signs* of the operations of God's Spirit are directly related. To put it in the terms of the question with which we began this discussion, what causes a person to *be* a Christian and what signs *identify* a Christian are inextricably related. In making this claim, Edwards, in effect, asserts an essential unity between justification and sanctification, a unity which the justification disputants in the 1630s in Boston and many modern justification disputants may not have fully appreciated.

The ground of this unity resides in the very nature of that which defines every person's "true religion," whether that religion is Christian or not, and to that discussion Edwards turns immediately in part 1 of *The Affections*. In fact, what Edwards actually does in part 1 is offer a definition of personhood, not in the sense of distinguishing a human being from a being that would not be called human but in terms of identifying exactly who any

---

[24] Ibid., locations 28869–28887.
[25] Ibid.

individual person actually *is*. Understood in this way, part 1 of *The Affections* sets a mammoth agenda. Some may question whether Edwards fully accomplishes his agenda here, but, without doubt, he lays an anthropological foundation, based directly upon his understanding of Scripture, and then he proceeds in parts 2 and 3 of *The Affections* to build upon that foundation his full and final answer to the question, what makes a person a Christian?

As he builds his case in part 1, Edwards takes into account all manner of earlier philosophical and theological arguments about human identity; Norman Fiering's work remains the best analysis of the scope of this ideological background of *The Affections*.[26] Stated simply, Edwards is asking, "What is it that makes me who I am?" In effect, Edwards considers the classical and the romantic answers and rejects both of them. According to the former case, I am not defined solely by what I think (though what I think is very important). According to the latter case, I am not defined solely by what I feel (though what I feel is very important). To anticipate where Edwards is going with this argument, neither right thoughts alone (orthodox theology) nor right experiences alone (religious passion) make me a Christian.

Many who have read part 1 of *The Affections* with great sympathy wish that Edwards had spent the time on this section that he did on similar issues in *Freedom of the Will*. Part 1 of *The Affections* needed more explication in order to make its arguments watertight. Edwards himself seems to have sensed that part 1 could have been clearer: "It must be confessed, that language is here somewhat imperfect, and the meaning of words in a considerable measure loose and unfixed, and not precisely limited by custom, which governs the use of language."[27]

But whatever its problems, part 1 certainly did not need anything more to make Edwards's fundamental argument clear. If we do not identify a person solely by what she thinks or solely by what she feels, how do we identify that person? In the language of

---

[26] Norman Fiering, *Jonathan Edwards's Moral Thought and Its British Context* (Chapel Hill, NC: University of North Carolina Press, 1981).
[27] "Treatise on Religious Affections," *WJE*, vol. 1, Kindle ed., locations 29010–290126.

the book from which Edwards took his fundamental insight, we identify a person solely by what she "seeks first" (Matt. 6:28–33). And what that person "seeks first," Edwards calls that person's "affections."

Further, Edwards goes on to argue, one's religion, whatever that religion, is always defined by one's affections:

> What has been said of the nature of the affections makes this evident, and may be sufficient, without adding anything further, to put this matter out of doubt; for who will deny that true religion consists in a great measure, in vigorous and lively actings of the inclination and will of the soul, or the fervent exercises of the heart?
>
> That religion which God requires, and will accept, does not consist in weak, dull, and lifeless wishes, raising us but a little above a state of indifference: God, in his word, greatly insists upon it, that we be good in earnest, "fervent in spirit," and our hearts vigorously engaged in religion: Rom. 12:11, "Be ye fervent in spirit, serving the Lord." Deut. 10:12, "And now, Israel, what doth the Lord thy God require of thee, but to fear the Lord thy God, to walk in all his ways, and to love him, and to serve the Lord thy God with all thy heart, and with all thy soul?" and chap. 6:4, 6, "Hear, O Israel, the Lord our God is one Lord: And thou shalt love the Lord thy God with all thy heart, and with all thy might." It is such a fervent vigorous engagedness of the heart in religion, that is the fruit of a real circumcision of the heart, or true regeneration, and that has the promises of life; Deut. 30:6, "And the Lord thy God will circumcise thine heart, and the heart of thy seed, to love the Lord thy God with all thy heart, and with all thy soul, that thou mayest live."[28]

In other words, returning to the justification question, when we ask, what makes a person a Christian? in either of its senses, we are asking about that which a person "seeks first." Exactly how this works receives Edwards's attention indirectly in part 2 of *The Affections*, and directly in part 3.

In the course of my teaching career, I have frequently been asked what I think about this or that religious phenomenon. For

---

[28] Ibid., locations 29048–29075.

example, about fifteen years ago, this was a regular question: "How should we view the 'Toronto Blessing'?" I won't try to name more recent such phenomena lest I unnecessarily raise red flags with readers. But whenever I have been asked such a question, my response has always been the same: "Go read—or reread—part 2 of Edwards's *Treatise on Religious Affections*, see what you think that material has to say to the question, and come back and we will talk specifically." My answer is not entirely intended to give me time to prepare an answer that is helpful rather than hurtful, though it is that. This answer also reflects my conviction that no one has ever done a better job than Edwards does in part 2 of identifying the factors which *are* often used to make such decisions but which *never* should be.

That, of course, has most often been the problem in justification debates and in other debates about the nature of the Christian life and the nature of the church. If Edwards's ultimate goal in *The Affections* was to provide guidelines for detecting "counterfeit Christianity," in part 2 he could be said to be discussing "counterfeit counterfeit detectors." Applied to the specific historical context in which he was writing, part 2 of *The Affections* examines many of the things on which both proponents and opponents of the Awakening were focusing attention but that really are not signs one way or the other with regard to the genuineness of the Awakening.

That is, in fact, the title of part 2: "Showing What Are No Certain Signs That Religious Affections Are Truly Gracious, Or That They Are Not." And Edwards lists twelve such *nonsigns*. Whether the affair in question is the Toronto Blessing or the activities of Anne Hutchinson or any one of a number of more recent controversial phenomena, the presence or absence of these twelve things does absolutely nothing to help us decide whether the particular phenomenon is, as Edwards would say, "genuinely gracious." The presence or absence of these twelve things reveals absolutely nothing about what is being "sought first" within the phenomena in question.

For example, "It is no sign that affections have the nature of true religion, or that they have not, that they have great effects on the body."[29] And this means, on the one hand, that:

> Great effects on the body certainly are no sure evidences that affections are spiritual; for we see that such effects oftentimes arise from great affections about temporal things, and when religion is no way concerned in them. And if great affections about secular things, that are purely natural, may have these effects, I know not by what rule we should determine that high affections about religious things, which arise in like manner from nature, cannot have the like effect.[30]

But Edwards quickly adds, "Nor, on the other hand, do I know of any rule any have to determine, that gracious and holy affections, when raised as high as any natural affections, and have equally strong and vigorous exercises, cannot have a great effect on the body."[31]

In some ways, this may seem obvious. But the church in both Edwards's day and ours still needs the lesson. For example, what one does or doesn't do with one's hands in worship is too often taken for a sure sign of genuine spirituality. Those whose worship is enthusiastic often interpret the stillness of other worshipers as a sure sign of spiritual deadness. Conversely, those whose worship embodies "decency and good order" often interpret the raised hands and clapping of other worshipers as mindless passion. Neither interpretation is necessarily correct. Stillness and quietness in worship may occur in the context of spiritual deadness, but they may also occur in the context of deep and profound reverence. Raised hands and clapping may occur in the context of mindless passion, but they may also occur in the context of fervent worship of the one true God.

But what exactly does this have to do with justification? One connection goes back to the double-faceted question with which we started: What makes a person a Christian? At the very least,

---

[29] Ibid., locations 29618–29625.
[30] Ibid., locations 29631–29650.
[31] Ibid.

the relevance of this *non*sign to the second sense of that question is clear. We cannot tell anything *certainly* about whether a person actually is a Christian by the bodily activity (or lack thereof) of that person in worship.

But what about the first sense of our question—do the *non*-signs identified by Edwards have any relation to the question of what *causes* a person to become a Christian? It may be difficult to see any relationship between the two with respect to the nonsign discussed above. But others of the nonsigns provide fascinating suggestions about a possible relationship.

Consider nonsign 3: "It is no sign that affections are truly gracious affections, or that they are not, that they cause those who have them to be fluent, fervent, and abundant, in talking of the things of religion."[32] And nonsign 5: "It is no sign that religious affections are truly holy and spiritual, or that they are not, that they come with texts of Scripture, remarkably brought to the mind."[33] Without question, these two nonsigns apply to the behavior of the "enthusiasts" in the Awakening. The ability to give moving testimonies (perhaps about the powerful bodily effects that had been experienced) replete with Scripture references, is no sign one way or the other that the person giving the testimony has genuinely experienced an act of God's justifying grace.

But in light of where Edwards does ultimately locate the answer to our question, it perhaps would not be too much to say that Edwards here, in nonsigns 3 and 5, refers to more than just the Awakening extremists. We must remember that Edwards asserted back in *Thoughts* that the greatest hindrance to the work of the gospel was the "censoriousness" of those who were fundamentally right in their ministries. We must remember his fairly negative comment about Martin Luther, the one through whom the Protestant church rediscovered the orthodox doctrine of justification. Is it possible that nonsigns 3 and 5 have relevance to those who are "fluent" in their theological orthodoxy and in their understanding and utilization of Scripture? To push this point to

---

[32] Ibid., locations 29696–29703.
[33] Ibid., locations 29834–29840.

an extreme, would it be accurate to suggest that, as a matter of fact, Satan himself knows the truth, the truth about justification and everything else? And yet, even if that is accurate, Satan is not himself a Christian; he is not himself justified.

At the very least, given what Edwards said in his justification sermons, it is clear that theological orthodoxy does not "cause" justification. Only God "causes" justification. To at least some degree, theological orthodoxy may be a "condition" of justification, but, if so, it is simply one of several conditions. Justification is certainly "by faith," but the faith by which justification *is* cannot be simply equated with our ideas about either faith or justification.

The entire point of part 2 of *The Affections* is that many things which are often used to define what makes a person a Christian should not be so used—not because these things are themselves bad or unimportant but because they can be counterfeited by Satan. One of the things that Satan can counterfeit is fluent talk about the things of religion. Fluent—and orthodox—talk about the things of religion is not a sign of the *absence* of justification. But it is not a definite sign of its *presence* either.

All of this brings us to part 3 of *The Affections*, the most important section of the most important book ever written by a human being.

In section 1 of part 3, Edwards lays the ontological foundation for the rest of his argument: "Affections that are truly spiritual and gracious, do arise from those influences and operations on the heart, which are spiritual, supernatural and divine."[34] In some ways, this "sign" that justification has happened is of limited benefit when observing another person. We can never be absolutely certain that another person has experienced "the transition from wrath to grace in history." But this does not make the sign unimportant. Indeed, without this sign, none of the others would be possible. To return to Edwards's sermons on justification, this first sign of gracious affections expresses in a new form Edwards's earlier argument that God and God alone is the cause of justification.

---

[34] Ibid., locations 30839–30846.

Here is a further statement to this effect:

> From these things it is evident, that those gracious influences of the saints, and the effects of God's spirit which they experience, are entirely above nature, and altogether of a different kind from any thing that men find in themselves by the exercise of natural principles. No improvement of those principles that are natural, no advancing or exalting of them to higher degrees, and no kind of composition, will ever bring men to them: because they not only differ from what is natural, and from everything that natural men experience, in degree and circumstances, but also *in kind*; and are of a nature vastly more excellent. And this is what I mean by supernatural, when I say that, *gracious affections are from those influences that are supernatural*.[35]

So Edwards continues to affirm that man can do nothing whatsoever even to begin to move in the direction of justification. It is God's work from first to last.

But immediately after the paragraph quoted above, Edwards begins to lay out the distinctive way in which he will connect the internal with the external, the cause with the condition. What is the key element of what God "causes"? This is one of the most crucial ideas in all of Edwards's theology:

> From hence it follows, that in those gracious exercises and affections which are wrought in the saints, through the saving influences of the Spirit of God, there is a new inward *perception* or *sensation* of their minds, entirely different in its nature and kind from anything that ever their minds were the subjects of before they were sanctified. . . . There is what some metaphysicians call a new *simple idea*. If grace be, in the sense above described, an entirely new kind of principle, then the *exercises* of it are also new. . . . Here is, as it were, a new *spiritual sense*, or a principle or spiritual sensation, which is in its whole nature different from any former kinds of sensation of the mind, as tasting is diverse from any of the other senses. And something is perceived by a true saint, in the exercise of this new sense of mind in spiritual and divine things, as entirely diverse from anything that is per-

---

[35] Ibid., locations 30973–30986 (emphasis in original).

ceived in them by natural men, as the sweet taste of honey is diverse from the ideas men get of honey by only looking on and feeling it.[36]

To return to a point made earlier, it is precisely here, in this section of part 3 of *The Affections*, that Edwards directly quotes Thomas Shepard's "Parable of the Ten Virgins."[37] Shepard's response to the antinomian controversy of his day, clearly a dispute over the nature and results of justification, helps to shape Edwards's response to the theological issues of his day, which included justification and many other matters as well.

The action God takes in moving a soul from the kingdom of darkness to the kingdom of light involves this provision of a "new spiritual sense," and *this sense is the one thing that Satan cannot counterfeit*. But as important as the existence of this sense is, the exact character or nature of this sense makes all the difference when we ask what makes a person a Christian.

Sections 2–4 of part 3 of *The Affections* provide Edwards's precise and superbly helpful description of this sense. I will provide a couple of appropriate quotations from these three sections and then suggest some implications.

Section 2 is entitled "The first objective ground of gracious affections is the transcendentally excellent and amiable nature of divine things, as they are in themselves, and not any conceived relation they bear to self, or self-interest." After a lengthy examination of the disturbing prevalence of various kinds of "self-interest" even in churches that are theologically sound, he makes this profound claim:

> Whereas the exercises of true and holy love in the saints arise in another way. They do not first see that God loves them, and then see that he is lovely, but they first see that God is lovely, and that Christ is excellent and glorious, and their hearts are first captivated with this view, and the exercises of their love are wont from time to time to begin here, and to arise primar-

---

[36] Ibid., locations 30979–30998 (emphasis in original).
[37] Ibid., locations 31478–31490.

ily from these views; and then, consequentially, they see God's love, and great favor to them. *The saint's affections begin with God*; and self-love has a hand in these affections consequentially, and secondarily only. On the contrary, those false affections begin with self, and an acknowledgment of an excellency in God, and an affectedness with it, is only consequential and dependent. In the love of the true saint God is the lowest foundation; the love of the excellency of his nature is the foundation of all the affections which come afterwards wherein self-love is concerned as a handmaid: on the contrary, the hypocrite lays himself at the bottom of all, as the first foundation, and lays on God as the superstructure; and even his acknowledgment of God's glory itself depends on his regard to his private interest.[38]

Section 4 is entitled, "Gracious affections arise from the mind being enlightened right and spiritually to apprehend divine things." Edwards begins this section with a crucial caution: "*Holy affections are not heat without light,* but evermore arise from some information of the understanding, some spiritual instruction that the mind receives, some light or actual knowledge."[39] But, of course, this caution, aimed primarily at those who would downplay the significance of objective truth, must be, and by Edwards is, balanced by his earlier caution: "But yet it is evident, that religion consists so much in the affections, as that without holy affection there is no true religion. *No light in the understanding is good that does not produce holy affection in the heart.*"[40]

And just exactly what does "holy affection in the heart" produce? That is the focus of Edwards's attention throughout the remainder of part 3. But before we move to a quick consideration of those matters which might be regarded as answers to the second sense of our question (How is a person recognized as being a Christian?), a bit more needs to be said about the significance of what Edwards has argued in sections 1–4 of part 3.

Perhaps that "bit more" could best be summarized by posing and answering yet another question, one that Edwards posed of

---

[38] Ibid., locations 31712–31725 (emphasis added).
[39] Ibid., locations 32082–32088 (emphasis added).
[40] Ibid., locations 29417–29422 (emphasis added).

himself many times. Why should I exercise faith in Jesus Christ? Or, for the Christian, why did I exercise faith in Jesus Christ? Or, for the session examining a candidate for church membership, why exactly did you trust Jesus Christ as your Savior? Edwards claims that if the answers to those three questions are focused *only* on what a person *gets* as a result of exercising faith in Christ, then the answers are likely to reflect "counterfeit Christianity." The natural person, according to Edwards and according to Scripture, is extraordinarily adept at doing all kinds of things out of "self-love." The natural person, therefore, is able to do many "Christian things" that "look like" genuine articles. But all of those things can be, and often are, counterfeited by Satan. Even faith can be counterfeited, and it likely is being counterfeited if the only things about which a professed Christian can talk when asked why she is a Christian are the benefits she receives—or thinks she will receive—as a result of her faith.

On the contrary, "The saints affections begin with God." But while quoting this part of Edwards's revolutionary sentence, we must not forget the remainder of it: " . . . and self-love has a hand in these affections consequentially, and secondarily only." Self-love *does* play a role in genuine faith. After all, many of the promises made in Scripture are for good things—unimaginably good things—that await the saints of God. These are real blessings, real benefits, and failing to recognize and appreciate them adequately, even in prospect, amounts to a failure to give God the honor and praise that he is due.

And that is the key to the "begin with" language above. The fundamental reason why I—and you—should exercise faith in Jesus Christ is because *he deserves it!* He is worthy of my faith; he is worthy of my worship; he is worthy of my praise. We exercise faith in Christ primarily and fundamentally in order to *give to* God, not to *get from* God. As we genuinely seek to give glory to God, the blessings roll in, but if we act as though we are giving just in order to get, grave spiritual danger awaits. Jesus, of course, said it best: "Seek first the kingdom of God and his righteousness," and, if we really do that, "all these things will be added to you" (Matt. 6:33).

But Christians in Edwards's day and in our own were/are masters at pretending to give just in order to get, and it was this subtle counterfeiting of Christianity that Edwards wrote *The Affections* to expose.

Something happens in the moment of transition from wrath to grace in history, something that totally reorients a person's being. It may be called regeneration or it may be called the provision of a totally new "relish for God." Whatever it is called, the new Christian has, for the first time, an ability to love God just for who he is rather than exclusively for what he can do for the Christian, an ability which, no matter how hard he tries, Satan can never counterfeit.

There are numerous ways in which Scripture gives expression to the multifarious aspects of this transition, justification being one of those. But all of those facets are rooted, as we saw earlier, in the union of the believer with Christ. The Lord, as it were, grafts the individual into Christ. This is the ground on which the believer is justified—Christ's active and passive obedience become the believer's because the believer is in Christ. Being in Christ also gives to the believer a relish for the beauty of God, a relish that has always described the attitude of the three persons of the Trinity toward one another.

This is Edwards's ultimate, mature answer to the ontological sense of the question, what makes a person a Christian? It also leads directly to his ultimate, mature answer to the recognition sense of that question. When, as we are sometimes called upon to do, we look at others, seeking to determine, for example, if they are genuine saints and should be admitted to the Lord's Supper, the most effective and accurate procedure is, according to Edwards, to examine the degree to which they are, like their Savior, fundamentally and primarily focused on maximizing the glory that is brought to God. When, as we actually do much more often, we look at our own spiritual lives, what we really are "seeking first" says a great deal about who we really are.

Sections 5 and following of part 3 of *The Affections* provide Edwards's detailed understanding of what "seeking first the kingdom of God and his righteousness" actually looks like in real life. All of these sections are extraordinarily important, but I will focus on just a few that seem most apropos to discussions of justification today.

In perfect harmony with his statements in *Thoughts* concerning "censoriousness," Edwards says in section 6:

> There is a sort of men, who indeed abundantly cry down works, and cry up faith in opposition to works, and set up themselves very much as evangelical persons in opposition to those that are of a legal spirit, and make a fair show of advancing Christ and the Gospel, and the way of free grace; who are indeed some of the greatest enemies to the gospel-way of free grace and the most dangerous opposers of pure humble Christianity. [At this point, Edwards, in a footnote, cites Thomas Shepard's "Parable of the Ten Virgins."] . . . Some, who think themselves quite emptied of themselves, confident that they are abased in the dust, are full as they can hold with the glory of their own humility, and lifted up to heaven with a high opinion of their abasement. Their humility is a swelling, self-conceited, confident, showy, noisy, assuming humility. . . . But he whose heart is under the power of Christian humility, is of a contrary disposition. If the Scriptures are at all to be relied on, such an one is apt to think his attainments in religion to be comparatively mean, and to esteem himself low among the saints, and one of the least of saints. Humility, or true lowliness of mind, disposes persons to think others better than themselves; Philippians 2:3, "In lowliness of mind, let each esteem others better than themselves." Hence they are apt to think the lowest room belongs to them.[41]

He continues in section 8:

> But here some may be ready to say, Is there no such thing as Christian fortitude, and boldness for Christ, being good soldiers in the Christian warfare, and coming out boldly against the enemies of Christ and his people? To which I answer, There doubtless is such a thing. The whole Christian life is compared to a warfare, and fitly so. And the most eminent Christians are the best soldiers, endued with the greatest degrees of Christian

---

[41] Ibid., locations 33045–33083.

fortitude. And it is the duty of God's people to be steadfast and vigorous in their opposition to the designs and ways of such as are endeavoring to overthrow the kingdom of Christ, and the interest of religion. But yet many persons seem to be quite mistaken concerning the nature of Christian fortitude. It is an exceeding diverse thing from a brutal fierceness, or the boldness of the beasts of prey. True Christian fortitude consists in strength of mind, through grace, exerted in two things; in ruling and suppressing the evil and unruly passions and affections of the mind; and in steadfastly and freely exerting, and following good affections and dispositions, without being hindered by sinful fear, or the opposition of enemies. But the passions that are restrained and kept under, in the exercise of this Christian strength and fortitude, are those very passions that are vigorously and violently exerted in a false boldness for Christ. And those affections that are vigorously exerted in true fortitude, are those Christian, holy affections that are directly contrary to them. *Though Christian fortitude appears, in withstanding and counteracting the enemies that are without us; yet it much more appears, in resisting and suppressing the enemies that are within us; because they are our worst and strongest enemies, and have greatest advantage against us.* The strength of the good soldier of Jesus Christ appears in nothing more, than in steadfastly maintaining the holy calm, meekness, sweetness, and benevolence of his mind, amidst all the storms, injuries, strange behavior, and surprising acts and events of this evil and unreasonable world. The Scripture seems to intimate that true fortitude consists chiefly in this: Prov. 16:32, "He that is slow to anger, is better than the mighty; and he that ruleth his spirit, than he that taketh a city." . . . *There is a pretended boldness for Christ that arises from no better principle than pride.*[42]

Edwards has not yet finished hammering at this attitudinal point. He concludes section 8 of part 3 with this statement:

And that all true saints are of a loving, benevolent, and beneficient temper, the Scripture is very plain and abundant. Without it, the Apostle tells us, though we should speak with the tongues of men and angels, we are as a sounding brass, or a tinkling cymbal" and though we have the gift of all prophecy, and understand all

---

[42] Ibid., locations 33659–33703 (emphasis added).

mysteries, and all knowledge; yet without this spirit we are noth-ing. *There is no one virtue, or disposition of mind, so often and expressly insisted upon, as marks laid down in the New Testament, whereby to know true Christians. . . . The Scripture knows no true Christians, of a sordid, selfish, cross, and contentious spirit. Nothing can be a greater absurdity, than a morose, hard, close, spiteful true Christian.*[43]

As Edwards finished section 8, so he begins section 9, which is entitled, "Gracious affections soften the heart, and are attended with a Christian tenderness of spirit. He continues:

All gracious affections have a tendency to promote this Christian tenderness of heart. . . . The less apt [the true saint] is to be afraid of natural evil, having his heart fixed, trusting in God, and so not afraid of evil tidings; the more apt he is to be alarmed, with the appearance of moral evil, or the evil of sin. As he has more holy boldness, so he has less of self-confidence, and a forward assuming boldness, and more modesty. As he is more sure than others of deliverance from hell, so he has more of a sense of the desert of it. He is less apt than others to be shaken in faith; but more apt than others to be moved with solemn warnings, and with God's frowns, and with the calamities of others. *He has the firmest comfort, but the softest heart: richer than others, but the poorest of all in spirit: the tallest and strongest saint, but the least and tenderest child among them.*[44]

Many more points could be made about the signs of truly gra-cious affections, especially with respect to the extended descrip-tion Edwards gives of what counts as "evangelical obedience." But one point will have to suffice. In section 11, Edwards writes, "Another great and very distinguishing difference is, that the higher gracious affections are raised, the more is a spiritual appe-tite and longing of soul after spiritual attainments increased."[45] In other words, one clear sign that a soul genuinely relishes God is that she has relish for more relish.

Edwards states it much more elegantly:

---

[43] Ibid., locations 33729–33786 (emphasis added). In this context, Edwards quotes Shepard's "Par-able of the Ten Virgins" numerous times.
[44] Ibid., locations 33914–33927 (emphasis added).
[45] Ibid., locations 34178–34185.

> The more a true saint loves God with a gracious love, the more he desires to love him, and the more uneasy is he at his want of love to him; the more he hates sin, the more he desires to hate it, and laments that he has so much remaining love to it; the more he mourns for sin, the more he longs to mourn for sin; the more his heart is broke, the more he desires it should be broke; the more he thirsts and longs after God and holiness, the more he longs to long, and breathe out his very soul in longings after God: the kindling and raising of gracious affections is like kindling a flame; the higher it is raised, the more ardent it is; and the more it burns, the more vehemently does it tend and seek to burn.[46]

Interestingly, however, this "relish for more relish" is not experienced as frustration by the Christian. It, in fact, provides a ground of assurance of salvation. No one relishes God perfectly; Edwards himself was painfully aware of his own failure to do so. But the ground of assurance is not that one relishes God completely as one should; the ground of assurance is that, however much one does relish God, one desires to relish him more. Returning to what Edwards said about the "new sense," it is only the person whom the Holy Spirit has savingly touched who even knows what "relish for God" is. Satan—and all others in the kingdom of darkness—neither knows nor cares anything about "relishing God." That a person desires to love God more is the surest sign that that person is, indeed, already a member of the kingdom of light, because the desire to worship and serve God is an absolutely noncounterfeitable desire!

How is worship and service of God expressed in the normal activities of life? By obedience to the law of God. Thus, Edwards begins section 7 of *The Affections* with these words: "Gracious and holy affections have their exercise and fruit in Christian practice." Not only so, but "*It is necessary* that men should be universally obedient."[47]

---

[46] Ibid., locations 34178–34191.
[47] Ibid., locations 34306–34326 (emphasis added). To get a sense of the power of the word "necessary" in this statement, see sect. 3 of part 1 of Edwards's *A Careful and Strict Inquiry into the Modern Prevailing Notions of the Freedom of the Will Which Is Supposed to Be Essential to Moral Agency, Virtue and Vice, Reward and Punishment, Praise and Blame*, locations 13052–13185.

It is just as *necessary* that men be obedient as it is that they relish God in the act of faith. In neither case does human behavior *cause* justification. The Holy Spirit alone is the *cause* of justification. But a relishing faith and an evangelical obedience are both essential *conditions* of justification. Why? Because the essence of the "transition from wrath to grace in history" is the Spirit's action in grafting an individual into Christ. Once a person is genuinely in Christ, it is inevitable that the person sees and acts differently than when he was not in Christ.

Being in Christ gives the person a new spiritual sense because Jesus himself has a relish for the other members of the Trinity that simply does not exist outside him. The one in Christ relishes with the relish of Christ himself.

Being in Christ produces evangelical obedience because, as Edwards and many others have taught, the law of God is nothing more or less than the objectification of the very nature of God. "I am the LORD your God," and therefore, "You shall have no other gods before me" (Ex. 20:2, 3). Therefore, when one is in Christ, one lives out who he is, and that is evangelical obedience.

Not perfectly, of course. Before the Spirit's touch, none of us were "able not to sin." After the Spirit's touch, we are "able not to sin," but, because of the kind of reality that Paul describes in Romans 5, we sometimes do sin. It will only be in the new heavens and the new earth that we will "not be able to sin." Edwards was not a perfectionist. He knew his Bible and his own heart well enough to avoid that heresy. The sign of a truly gracious Christian is not that he never sins; the sign of a truly gracious Christian is that he truly relishes his God and, therefore, genuinely anguishes over any sin that he does commit.

Any sin! Edwards's understanding of the scope of that phrase can be fully appreciated only by a careful examination of his work on original sin, especially his comments in section 5 of part 1, where he discusses the frightening extent of our sins of *omission*: "The sum of our duty to God, required in his law, is *love*; taking love in a large sense for the true regard of our hearts to God, implying esteem, honour, benevolence, gratitude, complacence, etc. . . . . It therefore appears from the premises, that *whosoever withholds more of that love or respect of heart from God, which his law requires, than he affords, has more sin than righteousness.*"[48] Obviously, all genuine Christians (including Edwards) experience a lot of anguish!

But the anguish is good; it is good in that it reveals what we desire—to relish God more and better, to love him and to obey him more completely. The anguish demonstrates that the Holy Spirit has touched us and has given us a "new spiritual sense."

This then may be a guide for us when we deal with others whose theologies or lives (or both) we perceive to be not fully honoring to the Lord, not fully in accord with the teaching of Scripture. It may be a guide for us particularly when we see a professed Christian whom we believe doesn't think the right things about justification or who doesn't live like a justified person.

We begin—or we *should* begin—all such interactions by remembering the anguish we have felt when (not *if*, but when) we have discovered our own tendencies to withhold from God the complete love and worship and service that his law requires. We also begin by reminding ourselves of warnings from Edwards, such as:

> All gracious affections have a tendency to promote this Christian tenderness of heart. . . . [The true saint] has the firmest comfort, but the softest heart: richer than others, but the poorest of all in spirit: the tallest and strongest saint, but the least and tenderest child among them.[49]

> That all true saints are of a loving, benevolent, and beneficient temper, the Scripture is very plain and abundant. There is no one virtue, or disposition of mind, so often and expressly insisted upon, as marks laid down in the New Testament, whereby to know true Christians.[50]

> The first and worse cause of errors, that prevail in such a state of things, is spiritual pride. This is the main door by which the

---

[48] Ibid., locations 23335–23348.
[49] "Treatise Concerning Religious Affections," *WJE*, vol. 1, Kindle ed., locations 33907–233927.
[50] Ibid., locations 33729–33735.

devil comes into the hearts of those who are zealous for the advancement of religion.[51]

Spiritual pride disposes persons to affect separation, to stand at a distance from others, as being better than they; and loves the show and the appearance of the distinction. But, on the contrary, the eminently humble Christian is ready to look upon himself as not worthy that others should be united to him.[52]

And here the first thing I would take notice of, is censuring professing Christians of good standing in the visible church, as unconverted. I need not repeat what I have elsewhere said to show this to be against the plain, frequent, and strict prohibitions of the word of God. It is the worst disease that has attended this work, and most contrary to the spirit and rules of Christianity, and of the worst consequences.[53]

Luther, the head of the reformation, was guilty of a great many excesses in that great affair in which God made him the chief instrument.[54]

Our "chief end" must always be the same—to maximize glory and honor to our "beautiful Savior." When we or others think or do anything that fails the maximizing test, our "relish of God" compels us to speak or to act or to do both. But "it is necessary" that such speaking or acting itself embody *all* of the things which Edwards says characterize genuinely gracious affections. Because *that* is what makes a person a Christian.

---

[51] "Thoughts on the Revival," *WJE*, vol. 1, Kindle ed., 39828–39840.
[52] Ibid., locations 39965–39971.
[53] Ibid., locations 40858–40876.
[54] Ibid., locations 39753–39759.

CHAPTER FIVE

Justification by Faith Alone? A Fuller Picture of Edwards's Doctrine

Douglas A. Sweeney[1]

Edwards's doctrine of justification has attracted more attention since Vatican II and the trend toward a "new perspective on Paul" than ever before in the history of Edwards scholarship.[2] During the two hundred years from Edwards's death (1758) to the election of Pope John XXIII (1958), only five scholars devoted much attention to this doctrine.[3] Only two of these examined it with criti-

---

[1] An earlier version of this chapter was published in *Jonathan Edwards as Contemporary: Essays in Honor of Sang Hyun Lee*, ed. Don Schweitzer (New York: Peter Lang, 2011). My thanks to Hans Madueme, Scott Manetsch, Ken Minkema, Adriaan Neele, and Don Schweitzer for helpful comments on the drafts of this revision.

[2] Although the leaders of Vatican II (1962–1965) did not devote sustained attention to the doctrine of justification, numerous scholars since its close have assessed its implications for Catholic-Protestant dialogue on justification. Perhaps the most important of these within the English-speaking world has been the Catholic ecumenical thinker, Harry J. McSorley, who published three crucial studies on historic Catholic-Protestant disagreements after the Council (focusing closely on the doctrine of the freedom of the will and its bearing on soteriological dogma): "Luther, Trent, Vatican I and II," *McCormick Quarterly* 21 (Nov. 1967): 95–104; "The Key Issue of the Reformation," *Dialog* 6 (Autumn 1967): 261–64; and *Luther: Right or Wrong? An Ecumenical-Theological Study of Luther's Major Work, The Bondage of the Will* (New York: Newman Press, 1969). The most important fruit of the ecumenical dialogue on justification by grace through faith in Christ has been the *Joint Declaration on the Doctrine of Justification* (1999), The Lutheran World Federation and the Roman Catholic Church (Grand Rapids, MI: Eerdmans, 2000). The so-called new perspective on Paul was pioneered by E. P. Sanders, *Paul and Palestinian Judaism* (Philadelphia: Fortress Press, 1977), and James D. G. Dunn, *Jesus, Paul, and the Law: Studies in Mark and Galatians* (Louisville, KY: Westminster John Knox Press, 1990). The best responses to their work by classically Protestant theologians are to be found in Stephen Westerholm, *Perspectives Old and New on Paul: The "Lutheran" Paul and His Critics* (Grand Rapids, MI: Eerdmans, 2004), and D. A. Carson, Peter T. O'Brien, and Mark A. Seifrid, eds., *Justification and Variegated Nomism*, vol. 2, *The Paradoxes of Paul* (Tübingen, GE: Mohr Siebeck, 2004).

[3] See the "Index of Subjects" in M. X. Lesser, *Reading Jonathan Edwards: An Annotated Bibliography in Three Parts, 1729–2005* (Grand Rapids, MI: Eerdmans, 2008), 682. But note that Jan Ridderbos, *De Theologie van Jonathan Edwards* (The Hague, NL: Johan A. Nederbragt, 1907), 234–52, discussed Edwards's doctrines of faith and justification at some length, suggesting a certain amount of resonance with Roman Catholic teaching and anticipating recent scholarly dialogue on the matter.

cal acumen.[4] Since the early 1960s, though, a host of people have studied it, engaging in what has become one of the most important interpretive conversations in the field. Some have suggested that Edwards harbored a quasi-Catholic view of the matter, one that smacks of Thomas Aquinas and the decrees of the Council of Trent.[5] Others have countered that Edwards held a consistently high Calvinist doctrine, presenting him as a Protestant conservative.[6] Still others offer less defensive mediating views, portraying Edwards as a Protestant while paying great respect to the metaphysical capaciousness that separates his thought from that of the Calvinist rank and file, makes his doctrine sound more catholic (though not really Roman Catholic), and renders him fascinating to humanists as well.[7] Nearly everyone who has published on this controversial issue, though, has limited him/herself to Edwards's well-known published discourse, *Justification by Faith Alone* (1738), along with a smattering of statements from his master's thesis at Yale and a few of the theological notebooks where he treated the

Lesser includes Ridderbos, but does not list his book as a treatment of justification. My thanks to Adriaan Neele for reminding me of Ridderbos's treatment.

[4] Ridderbos, *De Theologie van Jonathan Edwards*, 234–52; and Thomas A. Schafer, "Jonathan Edwards and Justification by Faith," *Church History* 20 (Dec. 1951): 55–67.

[5] In addition to the article by Schafer cited above (written before Vatican II), see Anri Morimoto, *Jonathan Edwards and the Catholic Vision of Salvation* (University Park, PA: Pennsylvania State University Press, 1995); Gerald R. McDermott, "A Possibility of Reconciliation: Jonathan Edwards and the Salvation of Non-Christians," in *Edwards in Our Time: Jonathan Edwards and the Shaping of American Religion*, eds. Sang Hyun Lee and Allen C. Guelzo (Grand Rapids, MI: Eerdmans, 1999), esp. 187–91; Gerald R. McDermott, *Jonathan Edwards Confronts the Gods: Christian Theology, Enlightenment Religion and Non-Christian Faiths* (New York: Oxford University Press, 2000), the full version of his argument; Gerald R. McDermott, "Jonathan Edwards on Justification by Faith—More Protestant or Catholic?" *Pro Ecclesia* 17 (Winter 2008): 92–111; Michael J. McClymond, "Salvation as Divinization: Jonathan Edwards, Gregory Palamas and the Theological Uses of Neoplatonism," in *Jonathan Edwards: Philosophical Theologian*, eds. Paul Helm and Oliver D. Crisp (Aldershot, UK: Ashgate, 2003), 139–41; and George Hunsinger, "Dispositional Soteriology: Jonathan Edwards on Justification by Faith Alone," *Westminster Theological Journal* 66 (Spring 2004): 107–20.

[6] See esp. John J. Bombaro, "Jonathan Edwards' Vision of Salvation," *Westminster Theological Journal* 65 (2003): 45–67; Jeffrey C. Waddington, "Jonathan Edwards's 'Ambiguous and Somewhat Precarious' Doctrine of Justification?" *Westminster Theological Journal* 66 (Fall 2004): 357–72; and Michael McClenahan, "Jonathan Edwards' Doctrine of Justification in the Period up to the Great Awakening" (DPhil thesis, University of Oxford, 2006).

[7] See esp. Brandon Withrow, "Jonathan Edwards and Justification by Faith," *Reformation & Revival* 11 (Spring 2002): 93–109, and (Summer 2002): 98–111; Sang Hyun Lee, "Editor's Introduction," in Jonathan Edwards, *The Works of Jonathan Edwards* (hereafter *WJE*), vol. 21, *Writings on the Trinity, Grace, and Faith*, ed. Sang Hyun Lee (New Haven: Yale University Press, 2003), 62–105; and Sang Hyun Lee, "Grace and Justification by Faith Alone," in *The Princeton Companion to Jonathan Edwards*, ed. Sang Hyun Lee (Princeton: Princeton University Press, 2005), 130–46. Conrad Cherry, *The Theology of Jonathan Edwards: A Reappraisal* (1966; rev. ed. Bloomington, IN: Indiana University Press, 1990), also deals rather extensively with justification by faith, presenting something of a mediating view.

doctrine famously. None has studied the full array of exegetical writings in which Edwards fleshes out his doctrine of justification further.[8]

In what follows, I seek to build upon the work of previous scholars, employing a wide array of understudied sermons and other manuscripts—such as Edwards's *Blank Bible* and extensive *Notes on Scripture*—to tell the rest of the story of Edwards on justification. These materials shed new light on the recent debates among the experts over Edwards's striking statements on this controversial doctrine. Most importantly, they show that it is impossible to understand these controverted statements without reading them in the context of their author's exegetical and pastoral priorities. Edwards was a preacher in a nominally Christian culture. He devoted most of his time to reading the Bible and writing sermons. His priorities were biblical, his instincts ministerial. He was a Calvinist, to be sure. But he tried to promote a Calvinist view of justification by faith alone without lulling unconverted and spiritually lax church adherents into a false sense of spiritual security. He also felt an obligation to preach "the whole counsel of God" (Acts 20:27), as the Puritans used to say, accounting regularly for the full range of biblical materials. He did so as a confessional Reformed theologian. I will demonstrate below that he was not quasi-Catholic. But as Robert Brown has written, Edwards's "use of the Bible needs to be taken into account when assessing the structure and content of his theological [work]." He wrote as "a self-consciously biblical thinker" almost all the time. To under-

---

[8] Edwards's "greatest hits" on justification are "Justification by Faith Alone," *WJE*, vol. 19, *Sermons and Discourses, 1734–1738*, ed. M. X. Lesser (New Haven, CT: Yale University Press, 2001), 147–242; his master's thesis "*Quaestio: Peccator Non Iustificatur Coram Deo Nisi Per Iustitiam Christi Fide Apprehensam*," *WJE*, vol. 14, *Sermons and Discourses, 1723–1729*, ed. Kenneth P. Minkema (New Haven, CT: Yale University Press, 1997), 55–66; a few of the statements on justification in his "Miscellanies" notebooks: *WJE*, vol. 13, *The "Miscellanies," a–z, aa–zz, 1–500*, ed. Thomas A. Schafer (New Haven, CT: Yale University Press, 1994); *WJE*, vol. 18, *The "Miscellanies" 501–832*, ed. Ava Chamberlain (New Haven, CT: Yale University Press, 2000); *WJE*, vol. 20, *The "Miscellanies," 833–1152*, ed. Amy Plantinga Pauw (New Haven, CT: Yale University Press, 2002); and *WJE*, vol. 23, *The "Miscellanies," 1153–1360*, ed. Douglas A. Sweeney (New Haven, CT: Yale University Press, 2004). Not many of these are given careful consideration, but see esp. 13:472, 476; 18:187–88, 223–24, 341–42, 344–46, 495, 510–12, 530–31, 543–46; 20:74, 84–85, 119–20, 324–25, 382–83, 479–81, 483–84; 23:107, 196, 506–43; and the material on justification in his "Controversies" notebook, *WJE*, 21:332–41. For a comprehensive assessment of the secondary literature on Edwards and justification, see the introduction to Christopher Atwood's excellent dissertation, "Jonathan Edwards's Doctrine of Justification" (PhD diss., Wheaton College, 2011).

stand his varied statements on the doctrine of justification we must reckon with his ministry of the Word.[9]

Edwards's Anti-Catholicism

It must be granted right away in our more ecumenical age that Edwards hated Roman Catholics—not personally, of course, but in the aggregate. No matter what one decides about the potential of his doctrine as a resource for contemporary ecumenical dialogue, it would be foolish and dishonest to suggest that Edwards himself ever intended to build a bridge to Roman Catholicism. He opposed the Catholic Church in a typically old-Protestant way.[10] In continuity with the Puritans, who suffered persecution at the hands of Catholic and quasi-Catholic Tudor and Stuart monarchs, he contended that the Roman Church was "antichrist," the eschatological "whore of Babylon." He prayed and worked for its demise. In a sermon preached twice on Revelation 14:3, he said, "[t]he Antichristian church, or the church of Rome, is . . . called the great whore, but the true [evangelical] church is represented [in Scripture] as the faithful spouse of Christ."[11] One finds similar

---

[9] Robert E. Brown, "The Bible," in Lee, *The Princeton Companion to Jonathan Edwards*, 89. See also Robert E. Brown, *Jonathan Edwards and the Bible* (Bloomington, IN: Indiana University Press, 2002). I have written at length on Edwards's ministry of the Word in *Jonathan Edwards and the Ministry of the Word* (Downers Grove, IL: IVP Academic, 2009).

[10] The tendency to label particularly heinous religious leaders as "the Antichrist" dates back to the tenth century (at least), and was entrenched in Western Christendom by the twelfth century. See Roberto Rusconi, "Antichrist and Antichrists," in *The Encyclopedia of Apocalypticism*, vol. 2, *Apocalypticism in Western History and Culture*, ed. Bernard McGinn (New York: Continuum, 1998), 287–325, who adds that "the individuation of Antichrist as referring to a specific pope and, finally, the identification of Antichrist with the very institution of the Roman papacy" itself took place gradually during the later middle ages (320). On early modern anti-Catholicism in Britain and her colonies (and on Britons calling the Roman Catholic Church "the antichrist"), see Christopher Hill, *Antichrist in Seventeenth-Century England* (London: Oxford University Press, 1971); Raymond D. Tumbleson, *Catholicism in the English Protestant Imagination: Nationalism, Religion, and Literature, 1660–1745* (Cambridge: Cambridge University Press, 1998); Thomas S. Kidd, "'Let Hell and Rome Do Their Worst': World News, Anti-Catholicism, and International Protestantism in Early-Eighteenth-Century Boston," *New England Quarterly* 76 (June 2003): 265–90; Thomas S. Kidd, *The Protestant Interest: New England after Puritanism* (New Haven, CT: Yale University Press, 2004); Geoffrey Plank, *Rebellion and Savagery: The Jacobite Rising of 1745 and the British Empire*, Early American Studies (Philadelphia: University of Pennsylvania Press, 2006); and Carla Gardina Pestana, *Protestant Empire: Religion and the Making of the British Atlantic World* (Philadelphia: University of Pennsylvania Press, 2009), esp. 159–217. As Julian Hoppit has noted well in *A Land of Liberty? England, 1689–1727*, The New Oxford History of England (Oxford: Oxford University Press, 2000), "Anti-Catholicism was one of the most potent ideologies in post-Revolution England, manifesting itself at all levels of society and sometimes in extreme forms" (221).

[11] Jonathan Edwards, *WJE*, vol. 22, *Sermons and Discourses, 1739–1742*, eds. Harry S. Stout and Nathan O. Hatch with Kyle P. Farley (New Haven, CT: Yale University Press, 2003), 227.

statements in dozens of texts throughout the Edwards corpus. As he summarized this sentiment to the Indians at Stockbridge just before the English attacked the Catholic forces of the French at Fort St. Frederic, Crown Point, on the shores of Lake Champlain, "[t]he religion of the Papists, that they [the French forces] are of, is contrary to God's word, and what he hates."[12] In that sermon and several others, he encouraged British Protestants to fight against the French and other Roman Catholic powers as "open enemies of God's church."[13] And in a startling note on Psalm 137, he suggested that the prophecy in verse 9 ("Happy shall he be, that taketh and dasheth thy little ones against the stones" [KJV]), fulfilled in part in ancient days, also looked "beyond the destruction of the literal Babylon to that of the spiritual Babylon [i.e. the Roman Catholic Church]. They indeed will do God's work," Edwards noted to himself, "and will perform a good work, who shall be God's instruments of the utter overthrow of the Church of Rome with all her superstitions, and heathenish ceremonies, and other cursed fruits of her spiritual whoredoms, as it were without having any mercy upon them."[14]

It needs to be said, furthermore, that Edwards opposed the Catholic Church mainly because he thought it misconstrued the gospel message itself, confusing people as to the doctrine of justification. He thought that Catholics taught salvation by our meritorious efforts, truly worthy good works, and he chided fellow Protestants who lived as though the Catholic Church was right about the matter. In a sermon preached at the onset of his minis-

---

[12] Jonathan Edwards, *WJE*, vol. 25, *Sermons and Discourses, 1743–1758*, ed. Wilson H. Kimnach (New Haven, CT: Yale University Press, 2006), 683.

[13] Ibid., 696.

[14] Jonathan Edwards, *WJE*, vol. 24, *The Blank Bible*, ed. Stephen Stein (New Haven, CT: Yale University Press, 2006), 537. For further introduction to Edwards's violent anti-Catholicism, see the sermon preached on July 10, 1746, a fast day for the British expedition to Canada (on Rev. 17:11, "And the beast that was, and is not, . . . goeth into perdition" [KJV]), box 12, f. 916, Jonathan Edwards Collection, Beinecke Rare Book and Manuscript Library, Yale University (hereafter Beinecke). Edwards argues there that "[Chris]tians should seek the overthrow of anti[christ] by using temporal means when called in provid[ence] to a temporal war with anti[chris]tian Powers. . . . The Countrey [. . . of Canada] belongs to the Kingd[om] of anti[Christ, . . .] the most considerable part of that Kingd[om] in These northern parts of America. . . . [I]f that Land was subdued[, it would] open a door for the Introducing the Gosp[el] into that dark Land" (L. 7v.–8r.). See the anti-Catholicism in *WJE*, vol. 24 (e.g., 24:365–69, 1227–29, 1235). N.B. My policy in what follows is to quote from Yale's letterpress edition of *The Works of Jonathan Edwards* when I can, offering literal transcriptions of the Edwards manuscripts not included in that edition.

try in Northampton (1729), he observed a harmful degree of cognitive dissonance on this theme. "There are probably hardly any amongst us," he warned his people,

> but what if they were asked whether they believed the popish doctrine of merit—that we could merit anything of God by our works—would say no. . . . But though they disown the doctrine in general, yet when they come to particulars, they plainly show that they do not disown it, but do think that God is obliged in justice to show mercy to them.[15]

In a sermon the following year, preached on Romans 4:16 (on God's promise to Abraham and his seed, received by faith), Edwards complained about Christians—Catholic, Protestant, and other—who held a high view of Scripture but a low view of the doctrine of justification it proclaims (i.e., Edwards's own doctrine). "[T]he Great Part of the Ch[urch] of Rome . . . deny this doc[trine]," he averred, "tis also vehemently opposed & Ridiculed by the Arminians."[16] If Arminians proved heterodox on justification by faith, just think how poorly Edwards thought of Roman Catholics. It is difficult to say this, and hurtful to belabor it, but Edwards had no interest in Catholic dialogue.

Edwards's Solifidianism

Edwards did maintain an interest in proclaiming the doctrine of justification by grace alone through faith alone in a classically Protestant way. Throughout his exegetical notebooks, he reminded himself that Scripture says "the freeness of God's grace" does not exist "at all for our righteousness."[17] Rather, "all are guilty, and in a state of condemnation, and therefore can't be saved by their own righteousness." Salvation only happens "by the righteousness of God through Christ received by faith alone."[18] In fact, one reason "why God suffered man to fall" from grace in the first place was

---

[15] WJE, 14:346.
[16] Jonathan Edwards, ms. sermon on Rom. 4:16 (1730), L. 8v., box 9, f. 692, Beinecke.
[17] WJE, 24:677.
[18] Jonathan Edwards, *The Works of Jonathan Edwards*, vol. 15, *Notes on Scripture*, ed. Stephen J. Stein (New Haven, CT: Yale University Press, 1998), 294.

"that he might see his . . . nakedness" and "be sensible of his absolute dependence on God for righteousness."[19] Therefore, Edwards argued, "we should not mingle the righteousness of Christ with our own righteousness," as he thought the Catholics did and feared that Protestants were all too often tempted to do as well, "or go about to cover ourselves partly with his righteousness and partly with our own, as though the garment of Christ's righteousness was not sufficient of itself to cover us and adorn us without being patched with our righteousness to eke it out."[20] The righteousness that saves comes entirely from the Lord, he said. Sinners never deserve it; saints appropriate it in faith and humble gratitude.

Edwards taught this doctrine publicly in scores of Sunday sermons. In a sermon on Hebrews 12:22–24 (1740), he said that "no man is Just in the sight of G[od] by his own Justice." Perfect righteousness is required by a perfectly holy God, he claimed, and none but God himself has ever abided by this standard. As he put this in the previously cited sermon on Romans 4, "When it is said [in the book of Romans that] we are not Justified by work[,] nothing else is implied, than that nothing that we do procures Justification of G[od] for us by virtue of the Goodness or Comeliness of it." Rather, God's saving mercy is bestowed because of Christ, whose perfect righteousness is imputed to those elected for this blessing. God's grace can make us holy. It does sanctify and improve us. Even the best human holiness, though, will never be enough to merit justification with God.[21] Speaking on Titus 3:5 (1729), Edwards systematized these teachings in familiar Protestant language, distinguishing the righteousness that justifies from that by which a sinner is sanctified:

> There is a two-fold righteousness that the saints have: an imputed righteousness, and 'tis this only that avails anything to

---

[19] *WJE*, 24:137.

[20] Ibid., 256.

[21] Jonathan Edwards, ms. sermon on Heb. 12:22–24 (1740), L. 2r.–v., box 11, f. 836, Beinecke; and Edwards, ms. sermon on Rom. 4:16, L. 7v. Careful readers will note that Edwards's sermon on Romans 4:16 anticipated similar language in "Justification by Faith Alone," *WJE*, 19:155. See also Jonathan Edwards, ms. sermon on John 5:45 (April 1741), box 8, f. 621, Beinecke, in which he says that "[t]he Law which natural men trust in to Justify 'em will only condemn 'em'" (L. 2v.).

> justification; and an inherent righteousness, that is, that holiness and grace which is in the hearts and lives of the saints. This is Christ's righteousness as well as imputed righteousness: imputed righteousness is Christ's righteousness accepted for them, inherent holiness is Christ's righteousness communicated to them. . . . Now God takes delight in the saints for both these: both for Christ's righteousness imputed and for Christ's holiness communicated, though 'tis the former only that avails anything to justification.[22]

Edwards spoke of faith itself in many other Sunday sermons, working hard to keep his people from defining it contractually as a set of affirmations that secured their justification. "Without faith it is impossible to please the Lord," he granted (Heb. 11:6). Faith is set forth in the Bible as a condition of justification (more on this below). It is not itself a work, however, that earns justification. Rather, faith is a gift of God by which a sinner clings to Christ, relying on Jesus and his work for justification. In Edwards's first publication, an oft-cited sermon with a standard Calvinist title, "God Glorified in the Work of Redemption, by the Greatness of Man's Dependence on Him, in the Whole of It" (1731), he characterized faith in just this theocentric way, waving the Calvinist banner high while keeping Christians from assuming that their faith was self-constructed and meritorious. Working from 1 Corinthians 1:29–31 ("He that glorieth, let him glory in the Lord" [KJV] etc.), he said that faith involves a "sensibleness" and "acknowledgment" of our "absolute dependence" on the Lord for justification. "Faith abases men, and exalts God," Edwards told his audience, "it gives all the glory of redemption to God alone."[23] This became a major theme in Edwards's homiletical ministry. To cite just one more instance from an understudied text, he said on Hebrews 13:14 (May 1733), "Faith it self don't Justifie because of [its] Hol[iness] or Goodness. . . . Tis not Respected of G[od] under that Consid[eration] when he Justifies

---

[22] *WJE*, 14:340–41.

[23] Jonathan Edwards, *WJE*, vol. 17, *Sermons and Discourses, 1730–1733*, ed. Mark Valeri (New Haven, CT: Yale University Press, 1999), 213.

man by faith[,] but only as it unites to [Christ.] Tis the thing by which the soul Closes with [Christ] & is united to him & so has an Int[erest] in him."[24]

This saving interest sinners have in Christ, and many other blessings of their union with the Savior, are detailed on countless pages of Edwards's exegetical writings.[25] Like John Calvin before him, Edwards grounded the imputation of Christ's righteousness to sinners on their real, mystical union with the resurrected Lord.[26] He did this famously, of course, in the published sermon on justification, claiming that "what is real in the union between Christ and his people, is the foundation of what is legal; that is, it is something really in them, and between them, uniting them, that is the ground of the suitableness of their being accounted as one by the Judge."[27] But he explored this theme beautifully in other places too. His many sermons on the canticles, which Edwards viewed as poetry on the intimacy of Christ and his elected earthly bride, overflow with carnal delight regarding the church's union with Christ and the benefits accruing to the saints

---

[24]Jonathan Edwards, ms. sermon on Heb. 12:14 (May 1733), L. 11v., box 11, f. 831, Beinecke. On the definition of faith and its role in justification, see also Jonathan Edwards, ms. sermon on Gal. 5:6 (Winter 1728), L. 4r.–7r., box 10, f. 767, Beinecke; Jonathan Edwards, ms. sermon on Hab. 2:4 (early 1730), L. 5v., box 6, f. 406, Beinecke; and, of course, the published sermon "Justification by Faith Alone," *WJE*, 19:149–50, 153, 156–58. These exegetical materials reinforce Edwards's teaching on the "natural fitness" of faith as a condition of justification, spelled out famously in his better-studied texts (see "Justification by Faith Alone," *WJE*, 19:159–60, as well as the "Miscellanies" and "Controversies," 18:187–88, 341–42, 344–46, 543–46; 20:119–20, 382–83, 479–81, 483–84; 21:339–40; and 23:196). Edwards taught in these well-known texts that sinners are saved by faith alone not because human faith is "morally fit" to secure a divine reward, but only because it is "naturally fit" that God should choose to employ faith as a condition, or the existential means through which the justified receive the gift of saving union with Christ. In numerous sermons, Edwards reinforced this teaching for his people, preaching that God is never obligated to compensate imperfect and inconstant human effort (whether in word or in deed) with the grace of justification, but has planned a way of salvation in such a naturally fitting manner, or existentially sensible way, that those who seek it usually find it. As he counseled in the aforementioned sermon on Titus 3:5 (1729), "A person may take encouragement from his own striving and diligence in seeking salvation. That is, he may think that there is more hopes, more probability, of his being converted because God enables him to strive, and with steadiness and constancy and earnestness to labor for salvation, than if he was dull and remiss and inconstant, and committed known sins and neglected known duties. For there is really a greater probability—though there be no certainty, yet there is a greater probability—that one that with great earnestness and diligence seeks salvation will obtain than one that is a negligent seeker" (*WJE*, 14:343).

[25]I have explored this theme at greater length in Douglas A. Sweeney, "The Church," in *The Princeton Companion to Jonathan Edwards*, 167–89.

[26]On Calvin and union with Christ, see the excellent book by J. Todd Billings, *Calvin, Participation, and the Gift: The Activity of Believers in Union with Christ*, Changing Paradigms in Historical and Systematic Theology (New York: Oxford University Press, 2008).

[27]*WJE*, 19:158.

therefrom.[28] For as he stated much more plainly in his sermons on the New Testament, Christ "is the great medium [and] head of union" with God, "[i]n whom all Elect Creatures . . . are united." And as he extrapolated later in another Sunday sermon, "[i]n the divine Transactions [and] dispensations relating to men's salvation[, Christ] and Believers are Considered . . . as one mystical Person. . . . Christ [and] his Elect Church are Respected as one . . . in the Purchase that [Christ] made" for her redemption.[29]

As suggested by the reference to his sermons on the canticles, Edwards thought that God's elect had *always* been saved by grace alone through faith alone because of the work of Christ on their behalf. Even before the incarnation, in the time of the Old Testament, the saints were saved by grace because of the Savior who was to come. As Edwards spelled out in the longest sermon series he ever preached—*A History of the Work of Redemption* (1739), based on Isaiah 51:8 ("my righteousness shall be for ever, and my salvation from generation to generation" [KJV])—ever since the fall of Adam "the sum and substance of both the Old Testament and New is Christ and his redemption. The religion of the church of Israel was essentially the same religion with that of the Christian church."[30] And as repeated in a lecture on June 4, 1740, the Old and New testaments, or old and new covenants, "are only the same Covenant of Grace in its old [and] new dispensation."[31] There had been progress in the knowledge of the gospel over time. The

---

[28] See, for example, Jonathan Edwards, ms. sermon on Cant. 5:3–6 (July 1737), L. 6r.–8r., box 4, f. 263, Beinecke; and Jonathan Edwards, ms. sermon on Cant. 2:3 (April 1746), L. 15r.–v., L. 16r., box 4, f. 259, Beinecke.

[29] Jonathan Edwards, ms. sermon on Eph. 1:10 (Jan. 1738/9), L. 3r., box 10, f. 769, Beinecke; and Jonathan Edwards, ms. sermon on Gal. 3:16 (Feb. 1756/6), L. 1v., 7r., box 10, f. 766, Beinecke. On this theme, see also Jonathan Edwards, "Sacramental Union in Christ" (Jan. 1751), a sacrament sermon on 1 Cor. 10:17, *WJE*, 25:585; Jonathan Edwards, ms. sermon on 1 Tim. 2:5 (after Feb. 1739), L. 3r., 5r. (and passim), box 11, f. 800, Beinecke; Jonathan Edwards, ms. sermon on Heb. 2:16 (Oct. 1745), L. 1v., 2r., 8r.–v., box 11, f. 818, Beinecke; Jonathan Edwards, ms. sermon on Heb. 12:29 (n.d.), L. 14v., box 11, f. 839, Beinecke; and Jonathan Edwards, ms. sermon on Rev. 12:1 (July 1741; repreached several times), L. 2r. (and passim), box 12, f. 906, Beinecke.

[30] Jonathan Edwards, *WJE*, vol. 9, *A History of the Work of Redemption*, ed. John F. Wilson (New Haven, CT: Yale University Press, 1989), 443.

[31] Jonathan Edwards, ms. sermon on Heb. 9:15–16 (June 4, 1740; Jan. 1753), L. 1r., box 11, f. 824, Beinecke. Edwards explored this theme more famously in his "Controversies" notebook, under the questions, "Wherein Do the Two Covenants Agree as to the Method of Justification, and the Appointed Qualification for It?" (*WJE*, 21:354–68), and, "In What Sense Did the Saints under the Old Testament Believe in Christ to Justification?" (*WJE*, 21:372–408). On these questions, see also Edwards's "The 'Miscellanies,' no. 1354," (*WJE*, 23:506–43).

Old Testament saints saw their Savior through a veil.[32] But the Messiah and his gospel had been typified, prophesied, and indicated constantly for centuries before the incarnation. Perry Miller notwithstanding, Edwards always proved himself to be a federal theologian.[33] He taught that Father, Son, and Spirit had agreed from all eternity to provide a way of salvation for humanity after the fall (the covenant of redemption). He taught that Adam was on probation while he lived in the garden of Eden: if he adhered to God's law, he and his progeny would have lived forever, walking with the Lord (the covenant of works). And Edwards affirmed that ever since the fall (which God allowed but did not will), sinners have had but one way of justification with God: by faith in the work of Christ, the "second Adam" of St. Paul (Romans 5; 1 Corinthians 15), who overcame the power of sin and death for those the Father gave him (the covenant of grace). This federal schema was a hallmark of the Calvinist tradition. First formulated in Heidelberg and codified for Puritans in the Westminster Confession of Faith (1647), it represented a very Protestant view of justification. Edwards used it all the time. At the beginning of his ministry to the people of Northampton (1729), he said "[t]he Covenant of Grace is that Covenant which G[od] has Revealed to man since he failed of life by the Covenant of works, Promising Justification & Eternal life to all that believe in J[esus Christ]." He said in another sermon on the cusp of the Great Awakening (1740), "[t]he Cov[enant] of Grace is . . . [Christ's] Last will [and]

---

[32] As he explained most fully in *A History of the Work of Redemption*, Edwards believed that during the centuries before the incarnation the gospel itself was "in a great measure hid under the veil of types and shadows and more obscure revelations," *WJE*, 9:366. But it was there for those with eyes to see—and many saw and believed. Indeed, though "[s]ome are ready to look on the Old Testament as being . . . out of date and as if we in these days of the gospel had but little to do with it," this "is a very great mistake, arising from want of observing the nature and design of the Old Testament, which if it was observed it would appear full of the gospel of Christ, and would in an excellent manner illustrate and confirm the glorious doctrines and promises of the New Testament" (*WJE*, 9:290).

[33] Perry Miller, *Jonathan Edwards* (New York: William Sloane Associates, 1949), 30–32, 76–78, denied that Edwards was a federal theologian, confusing generations of scholars. For more on the federal theology, pioneered in Heidelberg in the early 1560s by Zacharias Ursinus and Caspar Olevianus, see David A. Weir, *The Origins of Federal Theology in Sixteenth-Century Reformation Thought* (New York: Oxford University Press, 1990); and Willem J. van Asselt, *The Federal Theology of Johannes Cocceius (1603–1669)*, trans. Raymond A. Blacketer (Leiden: Brill, 2001). On Edwards's relationship to it, see Carl W. Bogue, *Jonathan Edwards and the Covenant of Grace* (Cherry Hill, NJ: Mack, 1975).

Testament," the "Condition" of which "is faith in Jesus Christ." And he employed the federal schema in a host of other places. He insisted to the end that justification in the sight of God had always been by grace alone through faith alone in Christ.[34]

Edwards's Catholic Language

Edwards also said some things, however, that sound less Protestant—especially to modern ears. Chronically frustrated by glib moral laxity in those the Lord had placed under his care, easy-believism and hypocrisy in Europe's state churches, and the struggle to help parishioners live up to the profession many had made during the heyday of New England's Great Awakening, he emphasized that true faith will always bear good fruit—that justification comes by faith alone but saving faith is never alone. He preached that genuine faith is always marked by acts of love. It always leads to good works. He even went so far as to say that only holy people are saved, that *final* justification is granted only to those who persevere in the faith and love that they profess. For understandable reasons, some interpret these claims as echoes of Roman Catholic teaching—but Edwards never did. In the remainder of this chapter, then, I shine a light on their place in his interpretation of Scripture and explain that he presented them in terms of traditional Calvinism.

Like many Protestant clergy serving Europe's state churches, Edwards often felt compelled to help his people understand that there is a difference between nodding to the truth of Christianity and living from a vibrant Christian faith. Indeed, even "the devils . . . believe, and tremble" (James 2:19 KJV), as he told his congregation (1746) and then preached before the Presbyterian Synod of New York (1752). "[F]or persons merely to yield a speculative assent

---

[34] Jonathan Edwards, ms. sermon on 2 Sam. 23:5 (Summer–Fall 1729), L. 4r., 3r., box 1, f. 77, Beinecke; and Edwards, ms. sermon on Heb. 9:15–16, L. 1v., 3r., Beinecke. For further exegetical instances of Edwards's firm commitment to the federal theology, see esp. Jonathan Edwards, ms. sermon on Gen. 3:11 (Feb. 1738/9), box 1, f. 2, Beinecke; Jonathan Edwards, ms. sermon on Gen. 3:24 (n.d.), box 1, f. 3, Beinecke; Jonathan Edwards, ms. sermon on Zech. 4:7 (n.d.), L. 2r., box 13, f. 1015, Beinecke; Jonathan Edwards, ms. sermon on Heb. 9:13–14 (Nov. 1738), box 11, f. 823, Beinecke; and Jonathan Edwards, ms. sermon on Heb. 12:22–24 (1740), box 11, f. 837, Beinecke. (There are several sermons in Edwards's series on Heb. 12:22–24, held in seven separate folders at the Beinecke.)

to the doctrines of religion as true, is no certain evidence of a state of grace," he claimed. Satan himself "is orthodox," so clearly orthodoxy by itself is not enough to save.[35] Or as he cautioned in an earlier sermon, preached in 1730, "There may be a sort of assent to the truth of the Gosp[el] without any true Grace[,] for the devils believe & tremble[,] & persons have a belief from Education & have the thing appearing Plausible & probable from moral Arguments. [B]ut these things will never make the soul have a sense of the Reality and Certainty of . . . the Gosp[el]." Edwards longed for his parishioners to sense this gospel certainty. "Let us not decieve [sic] our selves," he pleaded with them earnestly, "by any kind of assent of the understanding to the Gospel without an answerable . . . symphonizing [of] the Inclination & will[,] & yielding of the . . . soul." He despaired about the prevalence in many parts of Christendom of transitory, temporary, hypocritical faith, the kind that often sprouted quickly in the hothouse of revival but then wilted when transplanted into the soil of daily life. After George Whitefield swept through town, sparking a revival (October 1740), Edwards preached a sermon series on the parable of the sower (Matthew 13), urging people not to be awestruck by Whitefield's obvious eloquence but to live as the kind of soil in which the Word can bear fruit. This series harkened back to sermons Edwards preached a few years earlier, shortly after his first revival ended in disaster. Using a text from Hebrews 10:38–39 (1736)—"Now the just shall live by faith: but if any man draw back, my soul shall have no pleasure in him" (KJV)—he explained that "temporary faith don't Justify[,] but in order to [justification] Persons must have that faith that is of a Persevering sort." Far too many prove inconstant in their faith, Edwards stated. We "[r]ead of them [in Scripture] that believe for a while[,] Luke 8.13[,] & we Read of them that Concerning faith make shipwreck[,] I Tim. 1.19." Let their weakness be your warning, Edwards urged his congregation. Persevere in faith, he said, and put to practice what we preach. In a sermon preached the same year on James 2:18 (1736)—"I will shew thee my faith by my

---

[35] WJE, 25:617.

works" (KJV), etc.—he suggested that "words are Cheap," and that "Godliness is more Easily feigned in words than in . . . deeds." Roman Catholic theologians often criticized Protestants for pushing "demon faith" (see James 2:19) as they declaimed on justification, paying lip service to grace without stressing that God bestows it to perfect people's lives. Edwards listened to this criticism and called for the kind of Protestant faith that makes a lasting difference in the world.[36]

Whenever Edwards took the time to limn the differences in Scripture between demon faith and vital, active, justifying faith, he made it clear that the latter changed a person's very being. In a sermon on Romans 4:16, he clarified that saving faith is a "sense and Conviction of the Reality & excellency of [Christ] as a saviour," a new spiritual sense that "Entirely Inclines & unites the heart to him." It involves "the whole soul," he said, with "every faculty entirely Embracing and acquiescing in the Gospel." In another Sunday sermon on Habakkuk 2:4 (1730), Edwards also spoke of faith as "acquiescence of the whole soul" to Christ and the gospel. It is "a Closing with [Jesus Christ] & . . . his salvation," Edwards

---

[36] Edwards, ms. sermon on Rom. 4:16 (1730), L. 4r., 10v., Beinecke; Jonathan Edwards, six ms. sermons on Matthew 13:3–7 (Nov. 1740; repreached in 1756), box 6, ff. 462–63, 465–467, and 469, Beinecke; Jonathan Edwards, ms. sermon on Heb. 10:38–39 (Sept. 1736), L. 4v., 9r., box 11, f. 826, Beinecke; and Jonathan Edwards, ms. sermon on James 2:18 (May 1736), L. 14v. and passim. On the difference between nominal/orthodox/transitory faith and genuine/vital/saving faith, see also Edwards's "Blank Bible" on James 2:14–26 (*WJE*, 24:1171); and Jonathan Edwards, ms. sermon on Gen. 1:27 (Aug. 1751), box 13, f. 934, Beinecke, in which he explained to Stockbridge Indians that after the fall of Adam "[men] had Reason [and] und[erstanding] left[,] yet that without Holiness does men no Good," warning that if one "has great understanding [and] is wicked he is so much the worse" (L. 2r.). Calvinists had long struggled to formulate a helpful doctrine of temporary faith as distinguished from saving faith. On this struggle in Calvin himself, see esp. John Calvin, *Institutes of the Christian Religion*, ed. John T. McNeill, trans. Ford Lewis Battles, 2 vols. (Louisville, KY: Westminster John Knox, 1960), 3.2.9–12; David Foxgrover, "'Temporary Faith' and the Certainty of Salvation," *Calvin Theological Journal* 15 (Nov. 1980): 220–32; Barbara Pitkin, *What Pure Eyes Could See: Calvin's Doctrine of Faith in Its Exegetical Context*, Oxford Studies in Historical Theology (New York: Oxford University Press, 1999), 136–40; and Randall C. Zachman, *The Assurance of Faith: Conscience in the Theology of Martin Luther and John Calvin* (1993; repr. Louisville, KY: Westminster John Knox Press, 2005), 181–83. For more on the context of Edwards's series on Matthew 13, see Ava Chamberlain, "The Grand Sower of the Seed: Jonathan Edwards's Critique of George Whitefield," *New England Quarterly* 70 (Sept. 1997): 368–85. On the disastrous end of Edwards's first revival, see esp. Jonathan Edwards, *A Faithful Narrative of the Surprising Work of God*, in *WJE*, vol. 4, *The Great Awakening*, ed. C. C. Goen (New Haven, CT: Yale University Press, 2006), 205–08. For the Catholic notion that Protestants taught a demon or devil's faith, see Robert Bellarmine, "De Justificatione," 1.14–15, in his *Opera Omnia*, vol. 1, part 1 (Naples, IT: Josephum Giuliano, 1858), 482–87. Edwards had access to this notion in the work of one of his favorite theologians, Francis Turretin, *Institutio theologiae elencticae*, 3 vols. (Geneva: Samuelem de Tournes, 1679–1685), 15.7–9, available in English as *Institutes of Elenctic Theology*, 3 vols., ed. James T. Dennison Jr. (Phillipsburg, NJ: P&R Publishing, 1992–1997), 2:558–68.

added—again, "with every faculty of the soul."[37] And in July of 1750, shortly after his ejection from the pulpit in Northampton but while still preaching supply for his now disaffected people, he reminded them that "[s]aving faith differs from . . . common faith in its nature, kind, and essence. . . . [I]n him that is in a state of salvation," Edwards elucidated, "faith produces another effect; it works another way: it produces a settled determination of mind to walk in a way of universal and persevering obedience."[38]

These more fulsome definitions have gotten Edwards into trouble. They have seemed to some observers to have verged on works-righteousness by sneaking good works into the faith by which we are saved. Edwards always pointed to faith itself as "the qualification which G[od] has a primary Respect to in Justifying men."[39] But he also said that godly love is implied in saving faith and so is spoken of in Scripture as a condition of salvation—not a condition that secures justification before God, but a condition without which one does not have genuine faith. He said this famously in his published sermon on justification by faith. In "one sense," he ruminated,

> Christ alone performs the condition of our justification and salvation; in another sense, faith is the condition of justification; in another sense, other qualifications and acts are conditions of salvation and justification too: there seems to be a great deal of ambiguity in such expressions as 'condition of salvation' . . . and I believe they are understood in very different senses by different persons. . . . [A]s 'tis very often (and perhaps most commonly), used; we mean anything that may have the place of a condition in a conditional proposition, and as such is truly connected with the consequent, especially if the proposition holds both in the affirmative and negative, as the condition is either affirmed or denied; if it be that with which, or which being supposed, a thing shall be, and without which, or it being denied, a thing shall not be, we in such a case call it a condition of that thing: but in this sense faith is not the only condition of salvation or

---

[37] Edwards, ms. sermon on Rom. 4:16, L. 3r.–v.; and Edwards, ms. sermon on Hab. 2:4, 3r.–v., Beinecke.
[38] *WJE*, 25:498, 508.
[39] Edwards, ms. sermon on Hab. 2:4, L. 5r.–v., Beinecke.

justification, for there are many things that accompany and flow from faith, that are things with which justification shall be, and without which it will not be, and therefore are found to be put in Scripture in conditional propositions with justification and salvation in multitudes of places: such are "love to God," and "love to our brethren," "forgiving men their trespasses," and many other good qualifications and acts. And there are many other things besides faith, which are directly proposed to us, to be pursued or performed by us, in order to eternal life, as those which, if they are done or obtained, we shall have eternal life, and if not done or not obtained, we shall surely perish.[40]

He reasoned similarly in unpublished sermons and private notebooks.[41]

Edwards spoke in great detail about the importance of good works, sometimes saying things that sound remarkably Catholic.[42] In a sermon on Hebrews 10:38–39 (May 1733), he said that "None will . . . be admitted to see [Christ] but . . . Holy Persons." Three years later, in a sermon on Hebrews 12:14, he added in no uncertain terms: "Perseverance in Holiness is absolutely necessary to salvation."[43] However, he was usually quick to clarify that perseverance in holiness derives ineluctably from a new disposition wrought in sinners at conversion. Edwards taught that in conversion God infuses saving grace into the souls of the regenerate in the person of his Spirit, who binds sinners to Christ, redirects their affections (attuning them to God), and begins to bear divine fruit in their lives. On the basis of this binding and the changes that it brings, God justifies sinners by imputing the perfect righteousness of Christ to their accounts. This is not a "legal fiction," as Catholic critics claimed, for imputation is really grounded on a sinner's union with Christ. It has appeared to some Protestants

---

[40] *WJE*, 19:152.

[41] See, for example, his ms. sermon on Rom. 4:16, L. 6r.–v.; "The 'Miscellanies,' nos. 412, 416, 670, 808, 859, and 996" (13:472, 476; 18:223, 510–12; 20:84–85, 324–25); and his "Controversies" notebook (*WJE*, 21:360–61).

[42] For up-to-date analysis, see Stephen A. Wilson, *Virtue Reformed: Rereading Jonathan Edwards's Ethics*, Brill's Studies in Intellectual History (Leiden, NL: Brill, 2005).

[43] Edwards, ms. sermon on Heb. 12:14, L. 2v., Beinecke; and Edwards, ms. sermon on Heb. 10:38–39, L. 2v., Beinecke.

to be too Catholic, though, as Edwards ties justification to infused grace, the new disposition it effects, and even the promise of a sinner's sanctification.[44]

Edwards offered little engagement with this Protestant concern in his sermons and biblical manuscripts. He did say, however, that neither holiness nor even a regenerate disposition—in themselves—ever justify. And inasmuch as some have been confused about this matter,[45] it may prove useful to quote him here. Edwards specified in his homily on Titus 3:5 (1729), "there are none saved upon the account of their own moral . . . goodness, or any qualification of the person, any good disposition of the heart, or any good actions." For those who missed the point, he added, "none [are] saved upon the account of any habitual excellency, . . . or any moral or religious habit obtained by frequent acts or any truly gracious habit."[46] Somewhat later, he insisted in a sermon on Hebrews 10 that perseverance is "not necessary to salvation as the Righteousness by which a Right to salva[tion] is obtained. . . . [Nor] is it that Qualification by which the saints become interested in that Righteousness." Rather, it is "necessary" only as an "Evidence of a title to salvation," or of a sinner's "Effectual Calling." As he said on Hebrews 12, "[f]aith alone Gives the Right to salvation[,] yet

---

[44] For Edwards on infused grace and the changes that it yields, see esp. Jonathan Edwards, "Treatise on Grace" (*WJE*, 21:165); and "The 'Miscellanies,' nos. p, 73, 626, and 629" (13:171, 242–43; 18:155, 157–58). Paul Ramsay, "Appendix IV: Infused Virtues in Edwardsean and Calvinistic Context" (Jonathan Edwards, *WJE*, vol. 8, *Ethical Writings*, ed. Paul Ramsay [New Haven, CT: Yale University Press, 1989], 739–50), remains a helpful introduction to this topic. Hyun-Jin Cho, "Jonathan Edwards on Justification: Reformed Development of the Doctrine in Eighteenth-Century New England" (PhD diss., Trinity Evangelical Divinity School, 2010), offers an up-to-date defense of Edwards's Calvinism in light of these polemical concerns. On Edwards and the new disposition of the regenerate, see Sang Hyun Lee, *The Philosophical Theology of Jonathan Edwards* (Princeton, NJ: Princeton University Press, 1988). On Edwards and the Spirit's role in binding sinners to Christ, see Robert W. Caldwell III, *Communion in the Spirit: The Holy Spirit as the Bond of Union in the Theology of Jonathan Edwards*, Studies in Evangelical History and Thought (Milton Keynes, UK: Paternoster, 2006).

[45] This understandable confusion is rooted in "Miscellanies" entries in which Edwards speculates about the salvation of converted people who never have a chance to exercise their dispositions in explicit acts of faith. See esp. "The 'Miscellanies,' no. 27b" (13:213–15), where Edwards hints that "the disposition is all that can be said to be absolutely necessary" to salvation. But in addition to the sermons quoted below on this matter, see Edwards's "The 'Miscellanies,' no. 819" (18:530–31); and Edwards's "Controversies" notebook, where he clarifies that "in the method of justification by the gospel, a person is justified before he has any habitual holiness, or any holiness as an established principle of action . . . the establishing holiness as an abiding principle of spiritual life and action is consequent on justification . . . . And in this sense, again, God justifies the ungodly as he justifies persons without any habitual holiness" (*WJE*, 21:371).

[46] *WJE*, 14:333.

. . . Living a Life of Holin[ess] is necessary to the actual Recieving [sic] [of] salv[ation]." Faith, in other words, "is that Qualific[ation] that is Primarily necessary in order to persons Coming to see [Christ,] for tis the very thing by which they are united to [Christ] and Come to have an Int[erest] in him. But none have that Faith but H[oly] P[ersons]." Again, as he phrased this in a sermon on Galatians 5:6, "tis only faith without works that Justifies[,] yet [the] [Chris]tian Religion secures Obedience to [God] and Good Works." The "proper work of faith in the heart is to Change and Renew the heart." Therefore, "they that say they have faith and don't bring forth . . . Good works are like the dry limbs of a tree that must be Lop[pe]d off." By definition, justifying faith is "faith that is accompanied by works."[47]

Edwards stressed the close relationship of faith and good works nowhere better than his sermon series, *Charity and Its Fruits* (1738), on 1 Corinthians 13—especially in the twelfth of fifteen sermons in that series, "Christian Graces Concatenated Together."[48] He suggested in that sermon that "the graces of Christianity are all linked together or united one to another and within one another, as the links of a chain; one does, as it were, hang on another from one end of the chain to the other, so that if one link be broken, all falls; the whole ceases to be of any effect."[49] Further, "[a]ll the graces of Christianity always go together, so that where there is one, there are all; and when one is wanting, all are wanting. Where there is faith, there is love and hope and humility. Where there is love, there is also trust; and where there is a holy trust in God, there is love to God."[50] Speaking about the links of faith

---

[47] Edwards, ms. sermon on Heb. 10:38–39, L. 3r., 4r.; Edwards, ms. sermon on Heb. 12:14, L. 12r., 10r.; and Edwards, ms. sermon on Gal. 5:6, L. 11r., 7v.–8r., Beinecke. See also Jonathan Edwards, ms. sermon on Rev. 3:12 (July 1740; August 1752), box 12, f. 894, Beinecke, on the difference between what Edwards calls "thorough Christians" and "hypocrite" or "almost Christians"; Jonathan Edwards, ms. sermon on Luke 7:35 (July 1747), box 7, f. 549, Beinecke, in which Edwards says in a play on words that "true saints justify the Gospel of Jesus [Christ]" (L. 1r.) by consenting to it fully in heart and life; Jonathan Edwards, ms. sermon on Matt. 13:8 (March 1752), box 13, f. 1033, Beinecke; Edwards's comment on John 16:27 in "Blank Bible" (*WJE*, 24:957); and, of course, Edwards's discussion of the twelfth positive sign of truly gracious religious affections (*WJE*, vol. 2, *Religious Affections*, ed. John E. Smith [New Haven, CT: Yale University Press, 1959], 383–461).
[48] *WJE*, 8:326–38.
[49] Ibid., 327–28.
[50] Ibid., 328.

and love in particular, Edwards claimed that 1 Corinthians teaches unflinchingly that "[f]aith promotes love, and love is the most essential ingredient in a saving faith."[51] He emphasized that faith and works are tightly linked, that is, because the Bible does the same. As he put this in a sermon in the summer of 1750, "There is a keeping God's commands that the Scripture from time to time speaks of as necessary to salvation, and always accompanying a title to salvation."[52]

These sermons raise yet another reputedly Roman Catholic element in Edwards's view of salvation. Like Thomas Aquinas before him, Edwards described Christian charity as the life and soul of faith, claimed that Christians differ greatly in the degree to which their faith is formed by charity or love, and said their status and rewards in heaven vary accordingly.[53] In "Christian Graces Concatenated Together," for example, he depicted "love" as "the soul of [faith], . . . its working, operative principle or nature."[54] He confirmed in a note written on James 2:26 that "love is included in the nature and essence of saving faith, yea, is the very life and soul of it, without which it is dead, as the body without the soul."[55] He went on to say, moreover, that the saints enjoy varying degrees of grace on earth—varying degrees to which their faith has been perfected—and thus varying rewards from God in heaven. All the saints receive the same "imputed righteousness," he said, but they differ in the amount of "inherent righteousness" attained (14:266–67). They are "made fit for [heaven]" before they go to be with God. And "[t]here is a Correspondence [and] agreem[en]t between the saints' Qualifica[tions and] their priviledges [sic]" in heaven. "God takes notice of all the . . . works of the Godly," he maintained, and "will abundantly Recompence them in heaven."

---

[51] Ibid., 329.

[52] *WJE*, 25:529.

[53] Many volumes have been written on this theme in Thomas Aquinas. Paul J. Wadell, *The Primacy of Love: An Introduction to the Ethics of Thomas Aquinas* (New York: Paulist Press, 1992), remains a helpful English-language introduction.

[54] *WJE*, 8:330.

[55] *WJE*, 24:1173. See the note in the "Blank Bible" at James 2:14–26 (*WJE*, 24:1171), where Edwards says that "the working nature of faith [is] the life and soul of it"; and the first *Charity* sermon, "Love the Sum of All Virtue," where he argues, "[a]ll that virtue which is saving, and distinguishing of true Christians from others, is summed up in Christian or divine love" (*WJE*, 8:131).

However, there are "different degrees of Glory [and] happ[iness]" in store for them, distributed "according to their works." Those distinguished by their piety, who "have shewn forth [Chris]tianity in the Genuine beauty of it[,] they shall have a special Reward above others. [T]hey shall have a Crown of Peculiar brightness [and] Lustre[, and] shall be higher in Glo[ry] than others."[56]

For Edwards, though, charity itself is uncreated. It is the Holy Spirit dwelling in and bearing fruit in the saints. It is fully actualized the moment that saving faith is exercised.[57] It does not become more virtuous, and certainly not more worthy of God's justifying grace, as a result of human striving. God requires all his people to cooperate with him, to increase in sanctification and reflect his love to others. They accomplish this, however, as they "walk by the Spirit" (Gal. 5:16) and "abide in" the Lord (John 15), letting God govern their hearts and bear divine fruit in their lives. For Edwards, there are levels of grace and laurels for the godly. When God rewards good works, though, he crowns his own gifts (1 Corinthians 3). For as Edwards said in reference to 1 Corinthians 12:4, 6 ("Now there are diversities of gifts, but the same Spirit. . . . There are diversities of operations, but it is the same God which worketh all in all" [KJV]):

> The graces of Christianity are all from the Spirit of Christ sent forth into the heart, and dwelling there as an holy principle and divine nature. And therefore all graces are only the different ways of acting of the same divine nature, as there may be different reflections of the light of the sun. . . . Grace in the soul is the Holy Ghost acting in the soul, and there communicating his own holy nature. As it is in the fountain, it is all one and the same holy nature; and only diversified by the variety of streams sent forth. . . . They are all communicated in the same work of the Spirit, viz. the work

---

[56] Jonathan Edwards, ms. sermon on Matt. 13:23 (June 1756), L. 3v., box 6, f. 473, Beinecke; Jonathan Edwards, ms. sermon on Col. 1:12 (Aug. 1756), L. 1r., box 14, f. 1117, Beinecke; Jonathan Edwards, ms. sermon on Col. 1:12 (Jan. 1748/9; Jan. 1753), L. 1r., box 11, f. 790, Beinecke; and Jonathan Edwards, ms. sermon on Rev. 14:13 (n.d.), L. 3r.–5v., box 12, f. 909, Beinecke. On heavenly rewards, see also "The 'Miscellanies,' nos. 671 and 793" (*WJE*, 18:223–24, 495).

[57] For more on Edwards's view of infused grace and love as uncreated, see Lee, "Editor's Introduction" (*WJE*, 21:46–53), who disagrees with his former student, Anri Morimoto, *Jonathan Edwards and the Catholic Vision of Salvation*, 41–50, interpreting Edwards more consistently as Lombardian rather than Thomist in the debate over created versus uncreated grace.

of conversion. There is not one conversion to bring the heart to faith, and another to infuse love to God, and another humility, and another repentance, and another love to men. But all are given in one work of the Spirit. All these things are infused by one conversion, one change of the heart; which argues that all the graces are united and linked together, as being contained in that one and the same new nature which is given in regeneration.[58]

Finally, and relatedly, though Edwards sounded Catholic when he spoke about the "final justification" of the saints, he also meant for *this* term to be understood in a Protestant and Calvinistic way. He rarely used the term publicly. But in his famous sermon on the doctrine of justification, in his "Miscellanies" notebooks, and in the *Blank Bible*, he suggested that the error of those who misinterpret James on the doctrine of justification—particularly the words of James 2:24, "Ye see then how that by works a man is justified, and not by faith only"—was that they failed to "distinguish . . . first and second justification. The first justification, which is at conversion, is a man's becoming righteous, or his coming to have a righteousness belonging to him, or imputed to him. This is by faith alone. The second is at judgment, which is that by which a man is proved and declared righteous. This is by works, and not by faith only."[59] This sounds initially like an echo of the decree on justification at the Roman Council of Trent.[60] It is important to remember, though, that final justification was, for Edwards, automatic in the lives of those justified savingly in the first place. True faith perseveres, he said: "The Love of true saints to J[esus Christ] is such that nothing can extinguish or overcome." Moreover, "[p]erseverance is Looked upon as naturally Performed in the first act of faith[,] because that first act is of such a nature as shows the Principle to be of a Persevering sort."[61]

---

[58] *WJE*, 8:332.

[59] *WJE*, 24:1171. See also Edwards, "Justification by Faith Alone," in which he said that "God in the act of final justification that he passes at the sinner's conversion, has respect to perseverance in faith, and future acts of faith, as being virtually implied in the first act" (*WJE*, 19:203); and Edwards's "The 'Miscellanies,' nos. 847 and 1188" (*WJE*, 20:74; 23:107).

[60] For the Latin with English translation, see *Decrees of the Ecumenical Councils*, vol. 2, *Trent to Vatican II*, ed. Norman P. Tanner (London: Sheed & Ward, 1990), 671–83.

[61] Jonathan Edwards, ms. sermon on Cant. 8:7 (Dec. 1746), L. 1r., box 4, f. 268, Beinecke; and Edwards, ms. sermon on Heb. 10:38–39, L. 4v., Beinecke.

As he argued in his thirteenth sermon on Christian *Charity* (1738), "Grace Never Overthrown," the "believer is already actually justified to life, and therefore God will not suffer him to come short of life. Justification is an actual acquittance of a sinner, a final acquittance from guilt, and deliverance from hell, and acceptance to a free title to life. But this is inconsistent," he said, "with a deliverance from hell, and abiding life being yet suspended on an uncertain perseverance."[62] Sometimes saving faith is weak and accompanied with doubt. But in the main, Edwards stated, the converted should be sure of their salvation. Whereas Catholics had been told that their assurance comes only at the rite of extreme unction, Edwards told people with a vibrant, saving faith to be assured right now because of what God had done for them.[63]

Conclusion

Edwards taught that only those who persevere in faith and love will go to be with God in heaven. But he also said that faith alone unites such people to Christ, whose perfect righteousness alone can satisfy the law's demands. Human righteousness is necessary, but only as a sign that one is savingly converted, united to the Savior—and only as the fruit of the Spirit's presence in one's life. All other righteousness, for Edwards, is counterfeit and vain. The Father justifies the saints because of their union with his Son, imputing the righteousness of Christ to them because the Holy Spirit really binds them to the One who paid the price for human sin, enabling them to reflect the goodness, truth, and beauty of God.

Edwards often sounded more Catholic than many Protestants do. Like medieval Roman Catholics, he ministered in a state church and felt a special burden to distinguish true religion from its harmful counterfeits. He may well prove to be a better bridge for Catholic-Protestant dialogue than many other Calvinists with different pastoral burdens. But he never intended this; he was stoutly

---

[62] *WJE*, 8:347.

[63] For further exegesis on this theme, see "I Know My Redeemer Lives," in *The Sermons of Jonathan Edwards: A Reader*, eds. Wilson H. Kimnach, Kenneth P. Minkema, and Douglas A. Sweeney (New Haven, CT: Yale University Press, 1999), 141–60.

anti-Catholic. Almost everything he said that sounds Catholic, furthermore—on the nature of saving faith, on the regenerate disposition, on the sinner's union with Christ, even on final justification—had been said by other early modern Protestants.[64] Indeed, Edwards's Calvinist tradition had almost always been diverse. And even the highest, strictest Calvinists had sought not a faith that is opposed diametrically to Roman Catholic teaching, but reformed by a fresh reading of Scripture. Those today who want to defend Edwards's Calvinist credentials need to recognize this point. Like many early Reformed Protestants, he valued catholicity—even as, especially as, he criticized the doctrines he opposed in the Catholic Church.

Edwards taught what he did for largely exegetical reasons. He was responsible for preaching through the whole counsel of God. He had to explain how the apostle Paul agreed with 1 John, the moral earnestness of the Gospels, and the second chapter of James. He thought these texts should be expounded in a canonically balanced way. He read the Puritan Thomas Manton, whose

---

[64] A few examples must suffice. On the nature of saving faith, see William Ames, *Medulla theologica*, I, iii and II, v, in which the Puritan defines faith as "an act of the whole man" (English trans. in William Ames, *The Marrow of Theology*, ed. John D. Eusden [Grand Rapids, MI: Baker, 1997; 1968], 80). On the regenerate disposition wrought in sinners by the physical infusion of special, sanctifying grace in the soul (logically) prior to the first act of justifying faith (and much else that has been thought to be unique in Edwards's theology), see Peter Van Mastricht, *Theoretico-Practica Theologia*, VI, iii (English trans. in *A Treatise on Regeneration*, ed. Brandon Withrow [Morgan, PA: Soli Deo Gloria, 2002]). On union with Christ, sanctification, and their relation to justification, see Calvin's *Institutes*, 3.16.1, in which he asks: "Do you wish, then, to attain righteousness in Christ? You must first possess Christ; but you cannot possess him without being made partaker in his sanctification, because he cannot be divided into pieces [I Cor. 1:13]. Since, therefore, it is solely by expending himself that the Lord gives us these benefits to enjoy, he bestows both of them at the same time, the one never without the other. Thus it is clear how true it is that we are justified not without works yet not through works, since in our sharing in Christ, which justifies us, sanctification is just as much included as righteousness" (English trans. in *Calvin: Institutes of the Christian Religion*, 2 vols., ed. John T. McNeill, The Library of Christian Classics [Louisville, KY: Westminster John Knox Press, 1960], 1:798). On final justification and/or double justification in the early modern period, see William A. Clebsch, *England's Earliest Protestants, 1520–1535*, Yale Publications in Religion (New Haven, CT: Yale University Press, 1964); W. P. Stephens, *The Holy Spirit in the Theology of Martin Bucer* (Cambridge: Cambridge University Press, 1970), 48–70; Dermot Fenlon, *Heresy and Obedience in Tridentine Italy: Cardinal Pole and the Counter Reformation* (London: Cambridge University Press, 1972), 53–61; Edward Yarnold, "*Duplex iustitia*: The Sixteenth Century and the Twentieth," in *Christian Authority: Essays in Honour of Henry Chadwick*, ed. G. R. Evans (Oxford: Clarendon Press, 1988), 204–23; Carl R. Trueman, *Luther's Legacy: Salvation and English Reformers, 1525–1556* (Oxford: Clarendon Press, 1994), 55, 102–04, 140–42, 167–68 (Trueman and many others disagree with William Clebsch about the Protestant orthodoxy of the early English Reformers on the doctrine of justification); Peter Stephens, "The Church in Bucer's Commentaries on the Epistle to the Ephesians," in *Martin Bucer: Reforming Church and Community*, ed. D. F. Wright (Cambridge: Cambridge University Press, 1994), 48; Alister E. McGrath, *Iustitia Dei: A History of the Christian Doctrine of Justification*, 2nd ed. (Cambridge: Cambridge University Press,

sermons on the book of James said this at the troublesome verse in 2:24:

> In the Scriptures there is sometimes a seeming difference, but no real contrariety. . . . God would prevent misprisions and errors on every side; and the expressions of Scripture are ordered so, that one may relieve another. . . . The Scripture hath so poysed and contempered all doctrines and expressions, that it might wisely prevent humane mistakes and errors on every hand; and sentences might not be violently urged apart, but measured by the proportion of faith.[65]

Like Manton, Edwards affirmed and taught the Westminster Confession. He was a Calvinist who meant it—or, better, a post-Puritan champion of Reformed orthodoxy[66]—but refused to settle tensions in the Bible one-sidedly. He believed that *both* Paul

---

1998), 221–25 (Stephens and McGrath disagree about the significance of Bucer's doctrine of double justification); Kelly M. Kapic, *Communion with God: The Divine and the Human in the Theology of John Owen* (Grand Rapids, MI: Baker Academic, 2007), 126–37; Korey D. Maas, *The Reformation and Robert Barnes: History, Theology and Polemic in Early Modern England* (Woodbridge, UK: Boydell Press, 2010), 42–49; and Johannes Vlak, *Eeuwig Evangelium of Leer der zaligheid* (1684) and *Trias dissertationum de operibus Dei*, as summarized in Herman Bavinck, *Reformed Dogmatics*, vol. 3, *Sin and Salvation in Christ*, ed. John Bolt (Grand Rapids, MI: Baker Academic, 2006), 534: "The first [justification] consists exclusively in the forgiveness of sins, is grounded in the death of Christ, and can be called a justification of sinners. But the second is a justification of the godly, is grounded in the personal evangelical righteousness that believers themselves work out in the power of the Holy Spirit when they begin to live according to the commandments of Christ, and consists in the bestowal of eternal life and the reward that is linked to good works." Edwards stood in a long and diverse line of moderate Calvinists in the Anglo-American world concerned to prevent antinomianism (without condoning Arminianism) and answer the persistent moral criticisms of Calvinism. See Geoffrey F. Nuttall, *Richard Baxter and Philip Doddridge: A Study in a Tradition*, Friends of Dr. Williams's Library, Fifth Lecture (London: Oxford University Press, 1951); Tim Cooper, *Fear and Polemic in Seventeenth-Century England: Richard Baxter and Antinomianism* (Aldershot, UK: Ashgate, 2001); David P. Field, *Rigide Calvinisme in a Softer Dresse: The Moderate Presbyterianism of John Howe (1630–1705)*, Rutherford Studies in Historical Theology (Edinburgh: Rutherford House, 2004); and John Coffey, "Puritanism, Evangelicalism and the Evangelical Protestant Tradition," in *The Emergence of Evangelicalism: Exploring Historical Continuities*, eds. Michael A. G. Haykin and Kenneth J. Stewart (Nottingham, UK: Inter-Varsity Press, 2008), 252–77.

[65] Thomas Manton, *A Practical Commentary, or an Exposition with Notes upon the Epistle of James. Delivered in Sundry Weekly Lectures at Stoke-Newington in Middlesex, neer London*, 3rd ed. (London: J. Macock for Luke Fawn, 1657), 337. Edwards owned this book and used it frequently (see *WJE*, vol. 26, *Catalogues of Books*, ed. Peter J. Thuesen [New Haven, CT: Yale University Press, 2008], 339, 424, 452).

[66] As I have tried to demonstrate here, Edwards's doctrine of justification did *not* place him beyond the pale of traditional Calvinism. Nevertheless, he was eclectic. He appropriated ideas and ways of speaking about theology that are broadly Reformed, catholic, not always strictly Genevan. As he wrote of his identity in *Freedom of the Will* (1754): "I should not take it at all amiss, to be called a Calvinist, for distinction's sake: though I utterly disclaim a dependence on Calvin, or believing the doctrines which I hold, because he believed and taught them; and cannot justly be charged with believing in everything just as he taught" (Jonathan Edwards, *WJE*, vol. 1, *Freedom of the Will*, ed. Paul Ramsay [New Haven, CT: Yale University Press, 1957], 131).

and James must have been correct, even though their statements differed on the doctrine of justification. In a note on Romans 2:13—"For not the hearers of the law are just before God, but the doers of the law shall be justified" (kjv)—he wrote that Paul and James "were of the same mind in the matter of justification, however their expressions seem to be opposite. Here [in Romans] the apostle Paul says the same thing that the apostle James means, when he says a man is justified by works, and not by faith only. It is doubtless the same thing that the apostle James meant, if we would explain him by himself, for he expresses himself elsewhere almost in the same words that Paul does here (James 1:22–23, 25 ['be ye doers of the word, and not hearers only . . . ']).''[67] If all the Bible was inspired (2 Timothy 3:16), all its contents must be true and must harmonize in spite of their apparent inconsistencies.

Edwards did theology as a Calvinistic pastor. He interpreted the Bible with confessional commitments. He believed that this was the best way to exegete its meaning. But he also tried to be clear about the parts of sacred Scripture that did not fit neatly in his system. He aspired above all to prove faithful to his God and to the people in his charge. And he believed that this required him to preach texts that tied genuine faith very tightly to a life of good works. Those who want to understand his view of justification by faith can do no better than to read his Sunday sermons on the topic. As he boiled down his doctrine for the Indians of Stockbridge in one of these addresses (1751), he epitomized much of what is covered at length above. "We can't be saved without being good," he urged his new charges,

> But 'tis not because our goodness is sufficient, or can do anything of itself. But 'tis because all whose hearts come to Christ will be good, and if men ben't good, their hearts never will come to

---

[67] *WJE*, 24:988–89. See also Edwards's ms. sermon on James 2:18, in which he suggested: "There seemed to be some mistaken Principles [and] Ill Practices Prevailing amongst those that that apostle [James] Immediately directed his Epistle to[,] arising from their misunderstanding [and] misimproving of the doc[trine] the apostle Paul had Insisted on of Justification by faith only. . . . There was some of them Looking on faith as all and Good works as nothing[,] did neglect good works [and] hence allow thems[elves] in several Ill Practices" (L. 1r., Beinecke). James's intention, Edwards claimed, was not to oppose Paul's doctrine but to correct the misunderstanding of Paul prevailing among his audience.

Christ. . . . They whose hearts come to Christ, they are joined to Christ, and so they belong to him and therefore are saved for his sake. . . . And the great reason why God is willing to save good men is not because of their goodness, or for anything they do—for they are sinful unworthy creatures—but because they are joined to Christ.[68]

This simple missionary herald was the real Jonathan Edwards, the heart of whose theology was biblical exegesis. For this literary artist, metaphysical theologian, moral prophet, college teacher, nature lover, and civic leader was primarily a minister of the Word.

---

[68] Edwards, "He That Believeth Shall Be Saved," in *The Sermons of Jonathan Edwards*, 115.

Index

Also Available from Josh Moody

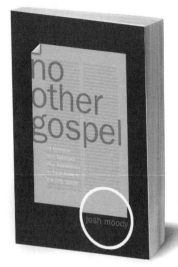

No Other Gospel
*31 Reasons from Galatians
Why Justification by Faith
Alone Is the Only Gospel*

"Paul's letter to the Galatians so strongly and passionately articulates the gospel of grace that it has proved transforming in many generations of preachers from Luther to Wesley and beyond. Here Josh Moody reinforces that heritage for the twenty-first century."

D. A. Carson, Research Professor of New Testament, Trinity Evangelical Divinity School

"These expositions are clear, well-organized, exegetically careful, and theologically faithful. They're also filled with good illustrations, personal application, and a proper dose of British wit. These qualities make for very good preaching and a very good book."

Kevin DeYoung, Senior Pastor, University Reformed Church, East Lansing, Michigan

"Pastor Josh Moody takes us verse-by-verse through Paul's letter to the Galatians. Along the way, he exposes our tendency toward man-exalting 'gospels' and then focuses our attention on the good news that exalts Christ. *No Other Gospel* is a model of compelling biblical exposition and a timely reminder to the church of the unchanging good news."

Trevin Wax, editor, LifeWay Christian Resources; author, *Holy Subversion: Allegiance to Christ in an Age of Rivals*